Collectables

Published in 2011 by New Holland Publishers (UK) Ltd
London • Cape Town • Sydney • Auckland
www.newhollandpublishers.com
Garfield House, 86–88 Edgware Road, London W2 2EA, United Kingdom
80 McKenzie Street, Cape Town 8001, South Africa
Unit 1, 66 Gibbes Street, Chatswood, NSW 2067, Australia
218 Lake Road, Northcote, Auckland, New Zealand

10 9 8 7 6 5 4 3 2 1

A catalogue record for this book is available from the British Library

ISBN 978 1 84773 966 7

Publisher: Aruna Vasudevan
Senior Editor: Jolyon Goddard
Editorial Assistant: Celia Turner
Cover and Inside Design: Colin Hall
Production : Melanie Dowland
Picture Editor: Susannah Jayes

Reproduction by PDQ Digital Media Solutions Limited, UK
Printed and bound in China by Toppan Leefung Printing Limited

Collectables
20th-Century Classics

NEW
HOLLAND

The 20th century was a period of truly inspirational and great design. The two world wars led to unprecedented population movement, in particular from Germany in the 1920s and '30s to Britain and America, and led talented designers such as Walter Gropius, head of Bauhaus, to work at British companies such as Isokon and later in the United States. Changes in production techniques, scientific advances and innovations in materials and industrial design also had an effect on how household wares were produced, making it possible for beautifully crafted products to reach mass markets at affordable prices. Processes and materials formerly used only in industrial or military design found their way into the production of domestic goods. Similarly, with changing and cheaper methods of travel, the world became an infinitely smaller place, enabling people to be aware of the design, colour, patterns, fabrics and materials commonly used in other countries. In particular, Scandinavian design began to seep into western European and American consciousness, resulting in a merging of techniques and the creation of even more inspiring furniture, lights, cutlery and so on.

Collectables: 20th-Century Classics has the rather ambitious task of showcasing almost 100 of the most desirable objects in the areas of furniture, household, lighting, glass and ceramics. Choosing what to include has been a monumental task. I hasten to add it is largely a personal selection of collectable items and mixes the truly expensive with the very affordable. It is by no means a comprehensive directory and thus I can already hear you saying: 'Why isn't *this* in the book?' and 'Why include *that*?' All I can say is, the items shown here are only a very brief insight into the wealth of influential but collectable 20th-century classic design.

To make the book easy to use, the items are arranged within colour-coded categories. Each entry features a photograph, often kindly supplied by the manufacturer, an essay putting the object and designer in context, some top tips on what to look out for and a website or two.

I hope this introduces you to or informs you about the world of the beautiful design objects on your doorstep, which men and women such as Marcel Breuer, Arne Jacobsen, Jessie Tait and the Eameses produced during the 20th century.

– Fletcher Sibthorp

Contents

Glass

Ceramics

B3 (Wassily) Chair
Marcel Breuer

Marcel Breuer developed the B3 Chair in 1925–6, while he was head of the carpentry workshop at the celebrated Bauhaus. The B3 was to become more popularly known as the Wassily Chair.

The seamless tubular steel of the Adler bicycle that Marcel Breuer rode around Dessau in Germany inspired him to develop a range of furniture from the same material. That wish, combined with the desire to design a chair supported by a single base – a cantilever chair – led to the B3. Both functional and comfortable, Breuer's chair was also stylish and modern. The original chair was made for just a few years before the outbreak of the Second World War in 1939. However, in the consumer boom following the war, there was a need for well-designed, mass-marketed furniture and the B3 went into production again. This time, it was made by Gavina in Bologna, Italy, and distributed through Stendig. The design was now marketed as the 'Wassily Chair', a reference to Breuer's friend, the artist Wassily Kandinsky, who had received an early prototype of the chair (made from canvas straps with a bent nickelled-steel frame). In the Gavina model, the straps were replaced by black leather and the frame was made of chrome-plated steel.

In 1968, US company Knoll bought both Gavina and the 'Wassily' name, but the design patent to the chair had expired. Knoll produces the official chair, but other companies also now manufacture this popular design.

☞ **Items to look out for**

The original B3 models, made of canvas straps and nickelled steel, are extremely hard to find.

If you're buying a licensed product, look for the Knoll stamp.

Top Tips

More modern versions are made of leather and chrome-plated steel.

It is still possible to find a Gavina-produced Wassily Chair, but most have been produced by Knoll (and cost about £1,250/US $2,000). There are, however, cheaper versions to be found for less than £310 (US $500).

Websites

Knoll
www.knoll.com

Also See

■ Isokon Long Chair, pages 22–3

LC3 Sofa (Grand Confort)
Le Corbusier/Jeanneret/Perriand

A stunning example of the collaboration between Le Corbusier, Pierre Jeanneret and Charlotte Perriand, the LC3, along with the LC2 and LC4, have become classics of design. The designers referred to them as 'cushion baskets'.

The LC2 and LC3 models are among the finest examples of modernist furniture; they were Swiss/French architect and designer Le Corbusier's response to the more traditional club armchair.

Immediately recognizable for its geometric form, which mixes leather and tubular steel, the LC2 was deemed uncomfortable by critics at the time (1920s). The LC3, by comparison, is all about comfort and has extra down-wrapped cushion pads, which are held in place but are not tethered to the steel frame.

The whole feel of the LC3 is softer and much more sumptuous, even though it still retains a somewhat industrial feel through the designers' use of high-gauge tubular steel frames that are externalized. The exterior frame is slightly wedged into the arms of the sofa and this helps achieve maximum comfort. The tubular frame also has chrome plating, which not only gives it a particular glossy shine but also makes it rustproof. The plating hides the joints, giving the sofa its classic seamless look.

The LC3 combines the industrial rationale and elegant minimalism of International Style with ultimate comfort. Today, the Italian company Cassina holds the licence to manufacture Le Corbusier-registered furniture.

☞ **Items to look out for**

The LC2 is more compact in design than the LC3.

🍷 **Top Tips**

More modern versions are made of aniline leather and highly polished tubular stainless steel frames.

If you're buying a licensed product, look for the Cassina stamp.

Real LC3s do not have joints on display.

Modern versions retail at about £680 (US $1,000).

🔲 **Websites**

Cassina
www.cassina.com

Also See

■ **Chaise Longue LC4,** pages 14–15

Chaise Longue LC4
Le Corbusier/Jeanneret/Perriand

The Chaise Longue LC4 was designed to evoke the shape and comfort of an 18th-century daybed. Today, it is viewed as a design classic.

In 1929, **Charles-Édouard Jeanneret-Gris** (better known as Le Corbusier), his cousin Pierre Jeanneret and the architect Charlotte Perriand unveiled the Chaise Longue LC4 at the Salon d'Automne in Paris. The LC4 was all about style and comfort.

The design has three main parts: a high-grade steel-coated base, a curved chrome-plated frame and a cushioned/padded leather mat with a headrest. The frame is adjustable, allowing the user to assume a variety of poses, from fully reclined to that of being upright. The chair's seat pad was upholstered in leather, although a variety of fabrics in different colours are available today. The LC4 came to epitomize what became known as International Style.

The chaise longue was produced from the late 1920s until the late 1950s. Le Corbusier, in collaboration with Swiss designer Heidi Weber, modified the design in 1959. The most significant adaptation was that the original elliptical tube base was replaced with a more readily available oval tube structure.

Only the Italian company Cassina makes authentic Le Corbusier-registered furniture, having been granted exclusive worldwide rights in 1964 by the Fondation Le Corbusier. However, there are many Le Corbusier-inspired models on the market today.

☞ **Items to look out for**

The original Le Corbusier/Jeanneret/Perriand design has an elliptical tube base and is upholstered in leather.

♥ **Top Tips**

Only **Italian company Cassina** has official licence to produce the LC4 and this retails at about £3,125 (US $5,000) and measures 56.4x160cm (22.2x63in). The frame is stamped with Le Corbusier's signature. The base is always black.

A faux LC4 retails at about £300 (US $480).

[www] **Websites**

Cassina
www.cassinausa.com

Also See

■ LC3 Sofa (Grand Confort), pages 12–13

Barcelona Chair
Mies van der Rohe/Reich

Originally for the German Pavilion at the 1929 International Exposition in Barcelona, the Barcelona Chair is a design classic and can be seen in museums, homes and offices all over the world today.

Modelled on the *sella curulis*, the stool favoured by ancient Roman magistrates, the Barcelona Chair is the product of a collaboration between acclaimed architect Ludwig Mies van der Rohe and interior designer Lilly Reich during the late 1920s. The chair was originally attributed solely to Mies van der Rohe, but in recent years Reich's contribution to its design has been acknowledged.

In 1929, the couple designed the low, tilted chair for the German Pavilion at the International Exposition in Barcelona. The Pavilion mixed marble, brass, glass and travertine to great effect and the Barcelona Chair's steel and leather thronelike design fitted it admirably.

The frame was originally designed to be bolted together and the pads were expensively finished in pigskin-leather. In 1950, the chair was redesigned to incorporate a seamless stainless steel frame and bovine leather replaced the pigskin.

The Barcelona was produced in limited quantities from the 1930s to '50s. In 1953, six years after Reich's death, Knoll acquired Mies van der Rohe's rights. Although Knoll continue to make the Barcelona Chair with Mies van der Rohe's name stamped on the frame, a number of excellent replicas exist on the market.

☞ Items to look out for

The original chairs combined reflective chrome with ivory pigskin.

♥ Top Tips

There are so many copies on the market today. The licensed Knoll version sells for upwards of £2,500 (US $4,000).

The Knoll version has a Knoll Studio logo and Mies van der Rohe's signature stamped into the frame.

▨ Websites

Knoll
www.knoll.com

Also See

■ **Brno Chair (MR50),** pages 18–19

Brno Chair (MR50)
Mies van der Rohe/Reich

A 20th-century design classic, the Brno Chair (MR50) was named one of the '80 greatest man-made treasures of the world' by English architecture guru Dan Cruikshank in 2005.

The MR50 is a modernist cantilever chair. It was designed by German-born architect Ludwig Mies van der Rohe in collaboration with German designer Lilly Reich in 1929–30 as bedroom furniture for the Tugendhat House in Brno, now in present-day Czech Republic. It has come to be known more popularly as the Brno Chair.

Influenced by the chairs of Dutch architect and designer Mart Stam, Mies van der Rohe and Reich combined clean, clear lines with comfort in the MR50. The original chair frame was made from a single piece of stainless steel that curved around into a C-shape to form the arms and legs and also bent under the seat to form the cantilever. An elegant, taut leather seat crowned the chair.

Today, the chair is available in both tubular and flat steel. It is officially licensed by Knoll, which calls them the Tubular Brno Chair and the Flat Bar Brno Chair. Knoll Studio's logo and Mies van der Rohe's signature are stamped into the frame. It is produced to the original specifications but can be purchased with or without arm pads and in more than 100 fabrics and 500 colours. Other producers also make and sell their own versions but the official chairs are made by Knoll.

☞ **Items to look out for**

The original MR50 model was made in stainless steel.

If you're buying a licensed product, look for the Knoll stamp.

💡 **Top Tips**

Modern versions are available in more than 500 colours.

While it is still possible to find original chairs, the modern versions sell from £660 (US $1,050) upwards.

🌐 **Websites**

Knoll
www.knoll.com

Also See
■ Barcelona Chair, pages 16–17

41 Paimio
Alvar Aalto

The 41 Paimio was designed by Alvar Aalto for the comfort of tuberculosis (TB) patients in the Paimio Sanatorium in Finland, which was completed in 1932. The chair's seamless design has made it a desirable object for collectors.

Alvar Aalto is one of the most celebrated exponents of Scandinavian design. His work is diverse, ranging from art glass to buildings and chairs. One of the items for which the designer is most famous is the 41 Paimio, a chair created in 1931 as part of a commission for the Paimio Sanatorium in southwestern Finland. Aalto designed the building, furniture and fittings for this TB hospital, work which helped establish his reputation.

Aalto believed that the furnishings and surroundings were as important to the patients' recovery at the sanatorium as their treatment. He aimed to design a building and environment that could serve as a 'medical instrument'. The sanatorium was full of light and had sun terraces, where the patients could relax.

Aalto experimented with wood, utilizing its pliant nature to produce a chair that would not just be comfortable but also would help ease a patient's breathing. The frame of the resulting 41 Paimio was made from single pieces of moulded birch plywood bent into closed curves with a single birch cross rail. The seat of the chair was made from one piece of birch plywood. Its flexible structure and the seat's angle made the chair highly comfortable. It is still produced by Artek, the company Aalto co-founded in 1935.

☞ Items to look out for

The original 41 Paimio can be found in museums around the world, such as the Museum of Modern Art (MoMA) in New York.

🍷 Top Tips

Artek manufactures the 41 Paimio. It can be bought in plywood lacquered in black or white and retails at about £2,570 (US $4,110).

🖥 Websites

Artek
www.artek.fi
SCP
www.scp.co.uk

Also See

■ Tea Trolley 901, pages 96–7
■ Savoy Vase, pages 172–3

Isokon Long Chair
Marcel Breuer

Marcel Breuer was one of the most influential furniture designers from the early 20th century. The Isokon Long Chair helped establish his reputation and also put the English firm Isokon on the world design map.

A 1930s' Isokon sales leaflet describes Marcel Breuer's elegant Isokon Long Chair as 'shaped to the human body. It fits you everywhere … These chairs have all the beauty of right design. Their lines express ease, comfort and well-being.'

Breuer designed the chair shortly after his arrival in England in 1936. Influenced by Bauhaus architect Walter Gropius, who was a consultant for the English company Isokon, Breuer came to work for the firm. Encouraged by Gropius to experiment in plywood and by Isokon owner Jack Pritchard to develop a chair based on his earlier 1932 Aluminium Lounge Chair for a mass-market audience, Breuer came up with the idea of making a chair that would fit or mould to the human form. The subsequent Isokon Long Chair had a bent frame of laminated birch wood, which supported a shaped timber seat and back. While the frames for the prototype were made in London, the bent seats came pre-made from the Venesta Plywood Company in Estonia. Along with the plywood chairs of Alvar Aalto, the Isokon Long Chair is one of the earliest examples of organic plywood furniture. It is credited with influencing designers such as Charles and Ray Eames in the post-war period.

☞ **Items to look out for**

The original models are rare and hard to get hold of but Isokon Plus makes modern reproductions.

The early models had a mortise and tenon joint.

Top Tips

Modern versions are available in birch, oak or walnut for £1,532 (US $2,450) or with a seat pad in Bute fabric for £2,022 (US $3,235).

Websites

Isokon Plus
www.isokonplus.com

Also See

■ B3 (Wassily) Chair, pages 10–11;
Isokon Penguin Donkey, pages 24–5;
Loop Table, pages 90–1

Isokon Penguin Donkey
Egon Riss

Designed by Egon Riss in 1939, the Isokon Penguin Donkey is a much sought-after piece of furniture. Only 100 of the original design were made.

Isokon was the brainchild of British furniture designer Jack Pritchard, who drew on his previous experience in the plywood business to build up what became one of the most forward-thinking design companies in Britain at the time. The company employed Austrian architect Egon Riss, who designed a bookshelf with Pritchard in the 1930s called the Donkey, so named because of its four legs and two panniers.

The use of a very thin sheet of plywood made the moulded, curvilinear shape of this bookcase possible. The central well, or middle section, was ideal for newspapers and magazines and the side plywood shelving was just the right size to house about 80 books. Pritchard came to an agreement with Allen Lane, founder of the publishing house Penguin, by which the Isokon Donkey was advertised in every book. The piece was subsequently renamed the Isokon Penguin Donkey. Both men believed that the Donkey would be a best-seller, but production ceased shortly after the outbreak of the Second World War.

In 1963, Ernest Race designed the Isokon Penguin Donkey Mark II. Mark III, designed by Shin and Tomoko Azumi for the successor company Isokon Plus, was released in 2003. Isokon Plus still makes an exact copy of the original design, using the original materials.

🖙 **Items to look out for**

The original Isokon Penguin Donkey was made of bent plywood. It was manufactured for a very limited period of time.

💡 **Top Tips**

More modern versions are made to the original specifications, but the original Isokon Penguin Donkey is still the most collectable. The price for a modern version is about £675 (US $1,080).

Websites

Isokon Plus
www.isokonplus.com

Also See

■ **Isokon Long Chair**, pages 22–3; **Loop Table**, pages 90–1

LCW (Lounge Chair Wood)
Charles and Ray Eames

The LCW proved the major breakthrough in the design career of husband-and-wife team Charles and Ray Eames. Affordable, comfortable and stylish, the LCW was perfect for the booming post-war market of the United States.

The Eameses created the LCW (Lounge Chair Wood) and DCW (Dining Chair Wood) in 1945, as part of a coded range of furniture intended to be affordable to most of the design-conscious post-war market.

Newly married, the Eameses had arrived in Los Angeles in the early 1940s. Charles Eames worked as a film set designer at the MGM Studio workshops. The couple's original designs used materials that Charles carefully smuggled out of MGM and involved experimenting with plywood, glue and rubber. The methods that the pair devised to mould wood at that time enabled the Eameses to create the range of revolutionary furniture for which they became famous, including the LCW, the chair that *Time Magazine* named 'the best design of the 20th century'.

The LCW is a masterly creation, combining comfort, style and innovation at what was an affordable price (today the chair commands thousands of pounds). Made up of a separate seat and backrest joined by a plywood spine, its low-slung form hugs the human body and the rubber shock mounts buffer against any jarring movement. Today, Herman Miller holds the Eames licence in the United States and Vitra has it for Europe and the Middle East.

☞ **Items to look out for**

The original 1945 plywood model.

When buying a licensed product, look for the official Herman Miller or Vitra stamp.

💡 **Top Tips**

Licensed models of the LCW are available in walnut (at about £485/US $779), natural cherry (£505/US $809), black and red (£570/US $909) and palisander (£800/US $1,279).

Miniature models are available from credible sellers so check what you buy!

🌐 **Websites**

Design Within Reach
www.dwr.com

Herman Miller
www.hermanmiller.com

Vitra
www.vitra.com

Also See

■ **La Chaise,** pages 36–7;
LAR, DAR and RAR, pages 38–9;
Soft Pad Chair, pages 82–3

NV-45
Finn Juhl

This beautiful and elegant chair designed by the Danish architect Finn Juhl for Niels Vodder was presented at the Copenhagen Cabinetmaker Guild Exhibition at the Danish Museum of Art and Design in Copenhagen in 1945.

Finn Juhl is considered by many to be the master of Danish furniture. He was the first Danish furniture designer to be recognized internationally. Like many of his peers, he started off studying architecture but he is known as a creator of high-quality, beautifully crafted sculptural furniture such as the NV-45 and Chieftain Chair.

In the late 1930s, Juhl began designing furniture primarily for his own use. By 1945, he had set up his own studio. It was Juhl's collaboration with master cabinetmaker Niels Vodder that brought him the most fame. The pair of craftsmen caused a stir at the annual Cabinetmaker's Exhibition with designs that were clearly influenced by modern, abstract art. At the Milan Triennials in the 1950s, Juhl was awarded five gold medals and won critical acclaim for his furniture.

The NV-45, or Model 45, is one of his most beautiful pieces of furniture. Conceived in 1945, it broke with the traditional idea of a chair design by freeing the seat and back from the frame. Upholstered in leather (or fabric), the chair has lovely curved moulded arms and sloping back legs made in high-quality teak, which showcase Juhl's attention to detail and his adherence to the use of only the best materials.

☞ **Items to look out for**

The original NV-45 stamped with 'Cabinet Niels Vodder' and 'Design Finn Juhl'.

💡 **Top Tips**

It is possible to pick up an original chair at auction at credible auctioneers such as Christie's for about £4,250 (US $6,800), but this model can go for as much as £6,875 (US $11,000).

🖵 **Websites**

One Collection: The House of Finn Juhl
www.onecollection.com

Skandium
www.skandium.com

Also See
■ **Chieftain Chair**, pages 40–1
■ **Teak Bowl**, pages 104–5

Round Chair
Hans J. Wegner

The Round Chair (Model 501) or simply 'The Chair' became part of US history when it was used in the first televised presidential debate between John F. Kennedy and Richard M. Nixon in 1960.

This elegant chair was created by Hans J. Wegner, one of the Danish designers who, like Finn Juhl, helped put furniture from this country on the world map. Wegner believed that furniture should be both functional and beautiful, and in his creations used natural materials to help make this possible. He was also incredibly prolific as a designer and has more than 500 chair designs to his name.

Wegner began his career as a cabinetmaker in the early 1930s, but he went on to study architecture in Copenhagen, after which he worked in the office of architects Arne Jacobsen and Erik Møller. By the early 1940s, Wegner had set up his own design studio and his attention to detail and excellent craftsmanship quickly won him fans. It was the Round Chair from 1949 that really established his reputation internationally, however. The chair's clean wood design is pared back to its bare essentials: a semicircle resting on four tapered legs with a cane or leather seat suspended between the legs.

The US magazine *Interiors* called it 'the world's most beautiful chair' and put it on its cover. When 'The Chair', as it came to be known, was used in the first televised US presidential debate it truly achieved cult status.

☞ **Items to look out for**

The original Round Chair can be seen in museums around the world.

Top Tips

A modern version of the Round Chair with a leather or woven seat can cost about £600 to £700 (US $960–1,120) if you are lucky.

Websites

PP Møbler
www.ppdk.com
Skandium
www.skandium.com

Also See

■ Wishbone Chair, pages 42–3;
  Teddy Bear Chair (PP19), pages 46–7;
  Valet Chair (PP250), pages 48–9;
  Oxchair, pages 70–1

Noguchi Table (IN-50)
Isamu Noguchi

Although possibly better known as one of the 20th century's most influential sculptors, Isamu Noguchi also created lighting, ceramics and furniture such as the iconic Noguchi Table in 1947.

Born to an American mother and Japanese father in California, Isamu Noguchi was raised in Japan until the age of 13. Moving to the United States, he lived with his family in Indiana, until he began to study medicine at Columbia University in New York. There, he took evening sculpture classes and discovered his true passion and gift. He eventually left university to concentrate on sculpture. After coming across the work of Romanian-born sculptor Constantin Brancusi, Noguchi moved to Paris to work with the great artist in the 1920s. There, he developed his own distinctive style, fusing modernism, elements of abstractism and emotional expressionism.

In the late 1930s, Noguchi's reputation in the United States escalated after he completed the first of several public-works sculptures for the Associated Press building in the Rockefeller Center in New York. In the 1930s, he also began to design interior goods for mass manufacture. His 1947 IN-50 glass table was put into production by Herman Miller and today remains a popular collector's item. Believing that everyday items could have sculptural input, Noguchi designed the glass and walnut coffee table to reflect the fluid lines seen in his sculptural work.

☞ **Items to look out for**

The walnut and glass table can cost upwards of £1,696 (US $2,710) at auction.

♟ **Top Tips**

More modern versions are still produced by Herman Miller in the United States and by Vitra in Europe and the Middle East.

🖥 **Websites**

Herman Miller
www.hermanmiller.com

Vitra
www.vitra.com

Womb Chair
Eero Saarinen

Spurred on by his protégée Florence Knoll's assertion that she needed a chair that she could curl up in, designer Eero Saarinen created the Womb Chair and its accompanying Womb Ottoman in 1948.

Finnish–American designer and architect Eero Saarinen always pushed the boundaries in terms of his designs, whether they be for a chair or a building such as an airport. The 1948 Womb Chair is no different and showcases Saarinen's design capabilities at their best. The chair provides ultimate comfort to the user while incorporating the best of contemporary design materials and techniques.

Saarinen, who worked with his friend Charles Eames in the 1930s to produce the Organic Armchair (the first armchair to be constructed out of moulded plywood), was classically trained in both architecture and sculpture. Both disciplines informed his subsequent designs for his interiors and exteriors.

The Womb Chair comprises a steel-rod base with a polished chrome finish and a fibreglass shell frame, which is covered in fabric. The shape of the chair is meant to tempt the user into a relaxed sitting position. Saarinen's aim was to create a chair that would by its design provide emotional comfort and a sense of security by making the user want to curl up in its warmth. Hence, it came to be known as the 'Womb Chair'. Saarinen designed a footstool, or ottoman, to accompany the chair.

☞ **Items to look out for**

An official Knoll custom-made Womb Chair and Ottoman can cost up to £2,190 (US $3,500).

Top Tips

Today you can buy the chair in three sizes: small, medium and large (on Knoll website below).

Websites

Knoll
www.knoll.com

Also See

■ Tulip Chair (Model 150), pages 56–7; Tulip Table, pages 58–9

La Chaise
Charles and Ray Eames

Charles and Ray Eames produced some of the most beautiful and influential furniture of the mid-20th century. The fluid, almost space-age lines of La Chaise make it stand out from their other designs such as the LAR, DAR and RAR.

The evolution of the idea for La Chaise came while the husband and wife Charles and Ray Eames were working with their friend designer and architect Eero Saarinen on plywood chairs for the Organic Design in Home Furnishings Competition held at the Museum of Modern Art (MoMA) in New York in 1947.

A year later, La Chaise was born. A startlingly dramatic piece of chair design, its fluid lines were inspired by the sculpture called Floating Figure by French artist Gaston Lachaise. MoMA had exhibited Lachaise's work in 1935. Lachaise's brass sculpture features a woman reclining but seemingly also floating in space; her body is attached to a pedestal. The likeness between the sculpture and La Chaise are quite remarkable.

The lines of the chair were made possible by technological advances in moulding fibreglass to create free-form shells for flexible seating. The chair essentially is two fibreglass shells fitted together and painted white. It has a chrome-plated tubular steel frame and a natural solid oak cross-shaped base.

Manufactured by Vitra, one of the pre-eminent names in European furniture, the chair has been made in limited quantities since 1991.

Items to look out for

La Chaise is now produced by Vitra. It can cost about £6,060 (US $9,700).

The early version had a rope or cord edge.

Top Tips

Look for seamless chairs. La Chaise is made to a high-quality specification and is an investment.

Websites

Design Within Reach
www.dwr.com

Vitra
www.vitra.com

Also See

- LCW (Lounge Chair Wood), pages 26–7; LAR, DAR and RAR, pages 38–9; ESU Bookshelf, pages 44–5; Model 670 and Model 671 (Lounge Chair and Ottoman), pages 60–1; Soft Pad Chair, pages 82–3
- Hang-It-All, pages 108–9

LAR, DAR and RAR
Charles and Ray Eames

Showcasing Charles and Ray Eames's desire to produce stylish but adaptable furniture to suit the changing needs of their target popular audience, LAR, DAR and RAR were a mix-and-match range of chairs from 1948.

In 1948, US designers Charles and Ray Eames developed a series of interchangeable mix-and-match components that could be made into different chairs. Their aim was to enter their creations into the Low Cost Furniture Design Competition held at New York's Museum of Modern Art (MoMA). They created seats, legs and bases of chairs that could be easily assembled or taken apart, using moulded fibreglass seats and metal rod bases.

The US car manufacturer Chrysler developed welded shock mounts to attach the fibreglass-reinforced plastic seats to the different bases. The resulting chairs included the DAR (Dining Armchair Rod) and LAR (Lounge Armchair Rod). The bases included the elegant Eiffel Tower-shaped legs, tapering metal-rod legs and the two carved pieces of curved wood that formed rockers for the RAR (Rocker Armchair Rod; see opposite). Initially available in grey, beige and grey-green, the chairs were manufactured by Herman Miller and Zenith Plastics (and the underside had a Miller–Zenith sticker in place).

LAR, DAR and RAR marked the first wave of mass-manufactured plastic chairs. Herman Miller gave a RAR to its employees when they had children.

☞ **Items to look out for**

Serious collectors look for the Miller–Zenith sticker on the underside.

🍢 **Top Tips**

Be careful when buying Eames products as there are many fake versions on the market.

▦ **Websites**

Herman Miller
www.hermanmiller.com
SCP
www.scp.co.uk
Vitra
www.vitra.com

Also See

■ LCW (Lounge Chair Wood), pages 26–7; La Chaise, pages 36–7; ESU Bookshelf, pages 44–5; Model 670 and Model 671 (Lounge Chair and Ottoman), pages 60–1; Soft Pad Chair, pages 82–3

■ Hang-It-All, pages 108–9

Chieftain Chair
Finn Juhl

Inspired by abstract painters and African sculpture, Finn Juhl created some of the most innovative and influential furniture of the 20th century. His classic Chieftain Chair was viewed as quite radical for its time.

One of Finn Juhl's most celebrated pieces of work, the Chieftain Chair was designed in 1949. Building on some of the principles explored in his earlier chair the NV-45 – separating the sculpturally shaped seat and back from the wooden frame – the emphasis of this design is in the chair's elegantly formed armrests.

The Chieftain Chair occupies a space filled with symbols inspired by weaponry and customs from foreign shores. Made by the very best craftsmen in teak and walnut, this piece is a chair that exemplifies grandeur and dignity.

Juhl was apparently influenced by African tribal art for the chair's design. Since its inception in the late 1940s, the Chieftain Chair has been produced by various Danish cabinetmakers. Manufactured originally by Niels Vodder in Denmark, the chair received its name when Danish King Frederik IX reportedly sat in the model on display at the 1949 Cabinetmaker's Guild in Copenhagen.

During a short period in the 1950s, Baker Furniture in the United States bought the licence to the Chieftain Chair design and produced a limited run. Today, the chair is a much sought-after item with collectors of inspirational furniture.

☞ **Items to look out for**

The original Chieftain Chair is a massive investment, if you can find one. It can retail from £7,190 (US $11,500) upwards.

💡 **Top Tips**

More modern versions are available in different colours.

Juhl designed a tiny table to go with the chair in 1965.

🌐 **Websites**

One Collection: The House of Finn Juhl www.onecollection.com
Skandium www.skandium.com

Also See

■ NV-45, pages 28–9
■ Teak Bowl, pages 104–5

Wishbone Chair
Hans J. Wegner

A love of natural materials and an understanding that furniture can be beautiful as well as functional have made Hans J. Wegner one of the most popular Scandinavian designers. His work appears in the world's leading museums.

Born in 1914 in Tønder, Denmark, Hans J. Wegner trained to be a cabinetmaker before studying at the Copenhagen School of Art and Crafts. He worked for Arne Jacobsen and Erik Møller before going solo in 1943.

Wegner's chair designs were made as stand-alone pieces and are beautiful objects in their own right. The designer believed that 'stripping the old chairs of their outer style and letting them appear in their pure construction' would help achieve this aim.

Of all his designs, the Wishbone Chair (or Y Chair), produced in 1949 for Carl Hansen and Son, is one of the most successful – and most copied. Wegner was influenced by portraits of Danish merchants sitting on Ming chairs and the Wishbone is one of his Chinese Chair Series. It mixes the old with the new: the steam-bending of timber and the weaving of cord seats with an original modern twist. Wegner collaborated on many of his designs with Johannes Hansen, a master cabinetmaker. Both men loved working with solid wood. It was certainly Wegner's material of choice when designing and something he deemed essential for making the perfect chair. 'The (perfect) chair does not exist,' the Danish designer famously commented. 'The good chair is a task one is never completely done with.'

Items to look out for

The Wishbone Chair is available in a range of timbers and colours. Prices begin at £445 to £550 (US $710–880).

Top Tips

The top rail of the original is one piece of steam-bent wood. Copies have two noticeable joins.

Auction sites, such as eBay, are good places to pick up Wegner chairs.

The older versions have a burned stamp instead of a sticker.

Websites

Carl Hansen and Son
www.carlhansen.com
Danish Furniture
www.danish-design.com

Also See

■ Round Chair, pages 30–1;
Teddy Bear Chair (PP19), pages 46–7;
Valet Chair (PP250), pages 48–9;
Oxchair, pages 70–1

ESU Bookshelf
Charles and Ray Eames

The Eames Storage Units (ESU) signified a new way forward, providing storage of the future, in which free-standing multifunctional shelving could be offered to a mass-market audience.

Always experimenting with design processes and materials, Charles and Ray Eames continued to build on the early successes of chairs such as LAR, DAR and RAR. Charles maintained that recognizing a need was a primary condition of design. Believing that general audiences could and should have well-designed functional goods at home in the post-war period, he understood that furniture could fulfil more than one use and also that the manufacturing techniques they were coming up with and the materials they were using could be put to a variety of uses. With that in mind, the Eameses and a group of like-minded individuals had designed leg splints, stretchers and aircraft parts made of moulded plywood for the US Federal Government during the Second World War.

After the war, the Eameses continued to experiment, using moulded plywood in mass-produced products. In 1949, they devised a new system of free-standing shelving which could be built strictly in keeping with the principles of industrial mass production. Made of galvanized metal surfaces, moulded movable plywood doors and brightly coloured screens, the Eames Storage Units (ESU) had adjustable legs and could be used for a multitude of purposes.

☞ **Items to look out for**

The ESU can cost upwards of £1,701 (US $2,720).

🍷 **Top Tips**

If you are buying through an unlicensed dealer, check their credentials carefully.

Herman Miller holds the licence for the ESU in the United States; Vitra holds it in Europe and the Middle East.

www **Websites**

Herman Miller
www.hermanmiller.com
The Conran Shop
www.conranshop.co.uk
Vitra
www.vitra.com

Also See

■ LCW (Lounge Chair Wood), pages 26–7;
La Chaise, pages 36–7;
LAR, DAR and RAR, pages 38–9;
Soft Pad Chair, pages 82–3

■ Hang-It-All, pages 108–9

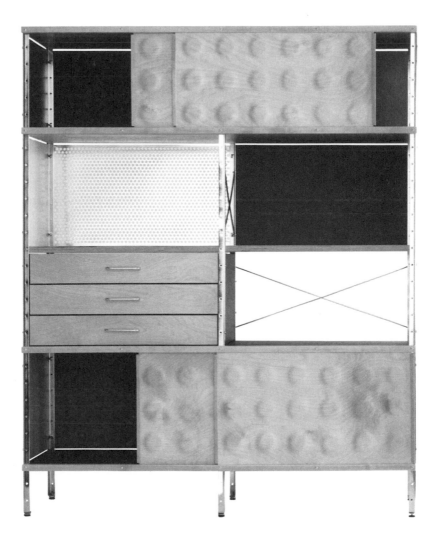

Teddy Bear Chair (PP19)
Hans J. Wegner

Master chair designer Hans J. Wegner produced more than 500 chair designs in his lifetime. The PP19, also known as the Teddy Bear Chair or PaPa Bear Chair, is one of his most popular – and is among his most desired by modern collectors.

Manufactured in the early 1950s, the PP19 was created both as a work of art and to support the human form. Like his other work, Wegner's lovely chair places comfort, ergonomics and functionality alongside beauty and craftsmanship.

The PP19 is both characteristically playful and organic in design. The chair received its name after a critic referred to its armrests as 'great bear paws embracing you from behind'. It is today better known as the Teddy Bear Chair and sums up the designer's belief that a chair should be beautiful from all sides and angles. Wegner also designed a footstool, known as the PP120, for the chair.

Originally manufactured by AP Stolen, the chair frames were supplied by the PP Møbler workshop, which would go on to produce Wegner designs in the late 1960s. The production of the chair resumed in 2003 to commemorate PP Møbler's 50th anniversary. It is also known as the PaPa Bear Chair.

Wegner received many international accolades for his influential designs during his lifetime. They include prizes from the Milan Triennials; an honorary doctorate from the Royal Society of Arts, London; and a Citation of Merit from the Pratt Institute, New York.

☞ Items to look out for

The Teddy Bear Chair can cost from £5,000 (US $8,000).

♟ Top Tips

The Teddy Bear Chair is also known as the PaPa Bear Chair.

The PP120 is the footstool that Wegner designed to go with the PP19.

▭ Websites

Danish Design Store
www.danishdesignstore.com

PP Møbler
www.ppdk.com

Also See

■ Round Chair, pages 30–1;
  Wishbone Chair, pages 42–3;
  Valet Chair (PP250), pages 48–9;
  Oxchair, pages 70–1

Valet Chair (PP250)
Hans J. Wegner

According to legend, fashion aficionado Karl Lagerfeld asked his parents for a Valet Chair as a young boy. Whether this is true or not, Hans J. Wegner's chair of 1953 is a masterly invention, combining simplicity and form with function.

Among Hans J. Wegner's most admired designs are the Peacock Chair (1947), which was inspired by the English Windsor chair and has a slatted backrest fanning out like a peacock's tail-feathers; the Folding Chair (1949), which could be hung on a wall; the Shell Chair (1948); and the Valet Chair (1953), which was designed to help hang or store a man's suit.

In many of Wegner's designs the quixotic mixes with the practical and the fun with the sublime. The PP250, or Valet Chair, is an example of this mixture. Reportedly conceived after Wegner had a conversation with architecture professor Steen Eiler Rasmussen and designer Bo Bojesen about the best methods of folding clothes at night-time, the Valet Chair is both functional and sculptural in form. The top rail is shaped as a coat hanger while the seat flips up to hang trousers. The seat also covers a box for storage of items such as keys, a wallet or cards – the kind of things one might store in suit pockets. The original prototype had four legs, but Wegner was dissatisfied with the look, deeming it too heavy. He continued working on the design and ended up removing one of the legs. The chair was originally made of teak and solid pine with leather and brass details. PP Møbler manufactures the Valet Chair today.

☞ **Items to look out for**

The original model is in demand. It was made of solid pine with an oiled teak seat. At a Chicago auction in 2010, an original sold for more than £13,125 (US $21,000); the estimate was £5,625 to £7,500 (US $9,000–12,000).

🍷 **Top Tips**

More modern reproductions are available, some made of ash.

Even a PP Møbler modern version doesn't come cheap at about £4,500 (US $7,200).

▦ **Websites**

PP Møbler
www.ppdk.com

Also See

■ **Round Chair**, pages 30–1;
Wishbone Chair, pages 42–3;
Teddy Bear Chair, pages 46–7;
Oxchair, pages 70–1

2-Seater Settee
Florence Knoll

Florence Knoll was a believer in the concept of Total Design. Through her own designs such as her Lounge Series and the designs of others manufactured by Knoll – the company she co-founded – Florence revolutionized 20th-century design.

A protégée of designer Eero Saarinen, Florence Knoll studied architecture at Cranbrook Academy of Art, the Architectural Association in London and at the Armour Institute in Chicago. She associated with and worked for a range of leading early 20th-century designers, including Walter Gropius and Marcel Breuer, who had been leading figures of Bauhaus. But it is in her capacity as co-founder (with husband Hans) of the extremely influential and successful Knoll Associates that Florence is probably best known.

Florence was concerned with creating modern interior and exterior products that were aimed at contemporary consumers – people with busy lives who were constrained by space limitations in the places where they lived and worked. Her 1954 Lounge Series, which featured the iconic 2-Seater Settee, was developed with this in mind. Angular but compact, the settee has a wooden frame and an exposed metal frame and legs made of heavy-gauge tubular steel. Although it is considered a design classic, Florence herself referred to it as 'meat and potatoes' and said that when she couldn't find similar furniture to suit her own needs she created it herself. The Knoll Lounge Series is still produced by the company.

☞ **Items to look out for**

The settee starts at £4,060 (US $6,497); it is part of a range including the 3-Seater Settee; 2- and 3-Seater Bonchos; and the Lounge Chair.

● **Top Tips**

There are many similar-looking settees but look for the official Knoll logo and Florence Knoll's signature stamped into the frame.

Websites

Knoll
www.knoll.com

Butterfly Stool
Sori Yanagi

Sori Yanagi worked with influential French designer Charlotte Perriand in her Tokyo-based practice. After setting up an industrial design institute, he designed the Butterfly Stool and Elephant Stool in the 1950s.

In about 1956, Sori Yanagi designed the Butterfly Stool, which consists of two molded plywood elements held together essentially by a metal rod. The Butterfly is so called because of its graceful curvilinear form, which is also reminiscent of a fleetingly jotted-down script character in Japanese calligraphy.

To create the stool, Yanagi used the same plywood-moulding techniques that husband-and-wife team Charles and Ray Eames invented in the 1950s to produce their mass-market furniture designs. Yanagi put together two identical moulded-plywood forms, which were held together by a simple brass stretcher. In creating the Butterfly Stool, which was originally made by Tendo Co., Yanagi meshed eastern and western aesthetics. In that same year, Yanagi also created the moulded Elephant Stool, which was originally manufactured by the Japanese firm Mokko. Today, the Butterfly Stool is produced by Vitra and has a maple or palisander veneer. An optional seat cushion in red Hallingdal upholstery fabric is also available.

The Butterfly Stool can be found in leading museum collections around the world, including the Museum of Modern Art (MoMA) and the Metropolitan Museum of Art, both in New York.

☞ **Items to look out for**

The Butterfly Stool retails from £400 (US $645) at Vitra-approved sellers. At auction, be prepared to pay several thousand pounds for an original.

Top Tips

The Butterfly Stool can be found on auction sites but check the credentials carefully.

Websites

Vitra
www.vitra.com

Also See

■ Teapot, pages 114–5

Model 3107 (Series 7)
Arne Jacobsen

Possibly one of the most copied chairs in the history of chair design, Arne Jacobsen's Model 3107 was conceived as part of his Series 7 group. Since its inception, the chair has sold more than five million copies.

Influenced by the idea that every element was important in the creation of truly good design – from the 'spoon to the city'– Arne Jacobsen strived to create perfection in every object or space that he designed. In the 1950s, his eyes turned increasingly towards industrial product design and he was particularly interested in the work and methods of the influential US design team Charles and Ray Eames.

Jacobsen began working on a series of chairs. The 3100 chair, produced in the early 1950s for the Danish pharmaceutical company Novo Nordisk, broke the mould of what good chair design should be. Made of a moulded-plywood frame set on three rather spindly-looking steel legs, the chair was immediately renamed the 'Ant'. That chair was arguably essential to the evolution of Model 310, the design for which Jacobsen is probably best known to popular audiences.

A compact, light hourglass-shaped plywood body on four steel legs, the Model 3107 was extremely comfortable to sit on. It was also attractive when viewed from any angle. The chair proved a runaway success, particularly after photographer Lewis Morley took a picture of Christine Keeler, of Profumo Affair notoriety, straddling it in 1963.

☞ **Items to look out for**

The original Series 7 chairs were hand produced. These are most collectable.

In 2005, Fritz Hansen started to make a children's version, exactly three-quarters the size of the original.

💡 **Top Tips**

Look out for the Fritz Hansen mark.

This is the most copied chair in chair design history. If you are paying £10 (US $16) it is most likely to be a fake.

The original chair has a 3D curve and no straight edges.

🌐 **Websites**

Design Within Reach
www.dwr.com

Fritz Hansen
www.fritzhansen.com

Also See

■ Egg Chair, pages 64–5;
Swan Sofa, pages 66–7

■ Cutlery, pages 116–7;
Cylinda Tea Service, pages 128–9

Tulip Chair (Model 150)
Eero Saarinen

Finnish–American designer Eero Saarinen believed in creating fluid, organic-looking furniture by using modern manufacturing techniques and materials. The Tulip Chair, made famous by its use on *Star Trek*, is an example of his approach.

Probably one of the most recognizable of Eero Saarinen's many designs, the Tulip Chair has reached iconic status not just for its futuristic design but also because it was used in the cult US television series *Star Trek* between 1966 and 1969.

Part of the last series of furniture that Saarinen designed, the Tulip is so named after the flower its lines so clearly resemble. Other critics have compared it to a wine glass. Either way, the Tulip Chair was the culmination of Saarinen's design concept of creating one piece from one material. Certainly it looks as if that is the case. In reality, the chair is made of fibreglass, aluminium and plastic. The shell seat is sculpted fibreglass and the stem has a fused plastic finish that covers the aluminium stem supporting the tulip-head seat.

In creating the chair, Saarinen wanted to design a clean, classic, uncluttered piece – a chair with a single leg instead of the mess of legs that created 'an ugly, confusing, unrestful world' in modern interiors, according to the designer. The pedestal base helped to produce the organic, neat, calm and elegant effect that Eero Saarinen so wanted to create for a popular audience.

☞ **Items to look out for**

The Tulip Chair dating from 1955–6.

The 50th Anniversary Collection produced by Knoll, which came with a commemorative medal and a certificate of authentication.

💡 **Top Tips**

You can buy the chair today with arms for £905 (US $1,446) and without arms for £825 (US $1,323).

If you're buying a licensed product, look for the Knoll stamp.

Websites

Knoll
www.knoll.com

Also See

■ **Womb Chair**, pages 34–5; **Tulip Table**, pages 58–9

Tulip Table
Eero Saarinen

Eero Saarinen became friends with Florence Knoll when they were studying at Cranbrook Academy of Arts in Michigan. Later, he came to design several classic pieces, including the Tulip Chair and Tulip Table, for the Knoll Studio.

'**Confusion comes** from trying to amalgamate several conflicting ideas,' Finnish–American designer Eero Saarinen once said. His designs reflect this thought, showing instead a clarity, simplicity and strength. Creations such as the Tulip Series successfully reveal a 'consistency and relatedness of all parts', ideas that Saarinen strove so hard to execute in his work. The designer believed that every piece of furniture had a 'holistic structure' and that everything should have formal unity.

In the mid-1950s, Saarinen designed the iconic Tulip Chair (Model 150), which was created to help make order in the chaos otherwise caused by the messy undercarriage of most tables and chairs. Instead, sporting a single elegant pedestal base, the Tulip was an elegant and minimalist design. The dining table that matched the Tulip Chair was similarly classic and sleek. It had a marble top covered in a transparent polyester coating, to help eliminate any stains, and a base made from cast aluminium, polished and coated in abrasion-resistant Rilsan.

Knoll released a commemorative version complete with medal and a certificate of authentication to celebrate the 50th anniversary of the collection.

☞ **Items to look out for**

The Tulip Table dating from 1955–6.

The 50th Anniversary Collection produced by Knoll, which came with a commemorative medal and a certificate of authentication.

● **Top Tips**

If you're buying a licensed product, check for the Knoll stamp. There are many copies products on the market.

In addition to marble you can choose granite or wooden top. The dining table with the Knoll stamp and Saarinen signature start at £2,916 (US $4,665).

▣ **Websites**

Knoll
www.knoll.com

The Conran Shop
www.conranshop.co.uk

Also See

■ Womb Chair, pages 34–5;
Tulip Chair (Model 150), pages 56–7

Model 670 and Model 671 (Lounge Chair and Ottoman) Charles and Ray Eames

Originally produced as a gift for US movie director Billy Wilder, the Lounge Chair and Ottoman were a great departure from the mass-manufactured products that Charles and Ray Eames had previously created.

Today a highly sought-after collector's item, the Model 670 chair, better known as the Lounge Chair and its accompanying (Model 671) Ottoman, were Charles and Ray Eames's take on the English classic club chair and footstool. Charles Eames said that he wanted to create a chair with the 'warm, receptive look of a well-used first baseman's mitt'. In the chair's squashed but sumptuous leather upholstery that makes anyone viewing it want to immediately sink down into its comfort, the Model 670 meets that end.

Charles and Ray launched the Lounge Chair during an interview in 1956 with Arlene Francis for the NBC programme *Home*, although it is notable that Charles is very much given the credit for their products – Ray is just referred to as Mrs Eames. Shrouded in darkness, the plywood, rosewood, leather and down-filled chair and ottoman were suddenly revealed in all their glory. In a very clever and slightly irreverent short movie set to music, the chair was seen being easily constructed from the base upwards, enjoyed by the man who had put it together and then deconstructed, only to end up back in a well-designed Herman Miller box.

☞ Items to look out for

The original model with a shell made from Brazilian rosewood.

♟ Top Tips

Still hand assembled, the shells are seven-ply cherry, natural cherry, walnut, or santos palisander. The chair and ottoman cost £4,777 (US $7,640) for the pair.

There are a plethora of cheap, low-quality copies, particularly from China.

▭ Websites

Herman Miller
www.hermanmiller.com

The Conran Shop
www.conranshop.co.uk

Vitra
www.vitra.com

Also See

■ **La Chaise**, pages 36–7;

Marshmallow Sofa
George Nelson

Nelson's influential designs could be seen in the more affluent households of 1950s' America. In 1956, he built on his already extraordinary success at furniture company Herman Miller by designing the Marshmallow Sofa.

Playful, whimsical and humorous are some of the words used to describe George Nelson's memorable Marshmallow Sofa. Nelson was one of the founding members of the modernist movement and through his company George Nelson and Associates worked with Herman Miller for more than 25 years. Nelson created his own designs for the company, such as the iconic Marshmallow Sofa and Action Office, and also brought the work of other designers, such as Japanese-American Isamu Noguchi, to the attention of the firm.

Made up of individual circular pads that can be removed, the Marshmallow Sofa had its origins in a cold call from a young industrial designer who had come up with a new cheap plastic disc. Nelson and Irving Harper (who had designed the Herman Miller logo) arranged several of the sample discs that the man had brought with him randomly on a frame. Although the meeting was not a success, the design that Nelson and Harper had so casually created stuck. Nelson devised the prototype for the Marshmallow, laying 18 circular discs on a tubular steel frame that made it look as if they were floating. The beauty of the sofa is that the cushions are detachable and so easy to clean. The owner can also mix the colours.

☞ **Items to look out for**

Marshmallow Sofa (1956): Herman Miller made only about 200 of the original Marshmallow Sofas, which now range between £7,500 and £11,250 (US $12,000–18,000) in price.

💡 **Top Tips**

More modern versions are available in a range of colours. The contemporary Herman Miller version retails at about £3,060 (US $4,899).

🌐 **Websites**

Herman Miller
www.hermanmiller. om

Also See

■ **Noguchi Table (IN-50)**, pages 32–3
■ **Sunburst Clock**, pages 98–9

Egg Chair
Arne Jacobsen

Jacobsen was a prolific and influential designer, producing everything from beautiful lighting and cutlery to his famous chairs, such as the Model 3017 (Series 7) and the classic Egg Chair.

Originally created in the late 1950s for the SAS Royal Hotel in Copenhagen, as were so many other iconic Arne Jacobsen designs, the Egg Chair is instantly recognizable and much knocked off in terms of faux versions (see Top Tips right).

Jacobsen's unique take on the traditional winged chair, the Egg Chair features a 360-degree swivel base. The seat is composed of upholstered foam and fibreglass. The base consists of a satin-polished, welded steel tube attached to an injection moulded aluminium cross. Originally intended for the lobby and reception areas of SAS Royal Hotel, the Egg Chair began its life as a plaster cast in Jacobsen's garage. The chair provides the user with a certain amount of privacy, the wings screening him or her from view. Jacobsen designed it with a matching ottoman – on a similar steel and aluminium base – and can be bought with or without it.

To celebrate the 50th anniversary of the Egg Chair in 2008, design company Fritz Hansen invited Israeli artist Tal R to cover 50 of Jacobsen's chairs. Choosing fabrics from all over the world, the artist chose to tell a variety of diverse stories through the fabrics he selected. The exhibition travelled around the world.

☞ Items to look out for

The original Fritz Hansen model sells for upwards of £3,750 (US $6,000). It is 110cm (43in) high, with taut fabric and a top-stitched single seam.

♟ Top Tips

There are several far cheaper but credible copies on the market for less than a quarter of the official price. Restoration Hardware, for example, sells the 1950s' Copenhagen Chair, which is 5cm (2in) higher than the original and has double roll and tuck seams.

🔳 Websites

Fritz Hansen
www.fritzhansen.com
Hive Modern
www.hivemodern.com

Also See

- ■ Model 3107 (Series 7), pages 54–5; Swan Sofa, pages 66–7
- ■ Cutlery, pages 116–7; Cylinda Tea Service, pages 128–9
- ■ AJ Light, pages 144–5

Swan Sofa
Arne Jacobsen

In the late 1950s, Danish architect and designer Arne Jacobsen created the Egg Chair, Swan Chair and Swan Sofa, among other designs, for the guests of the SAS Royal Hotel in Copenhagen.

A classic and instantly recognizable Arne Jacobsen design, the Swan Sofa, like its brother Swan and Egg Chairs, was created for the magnificent SAS Royal Hotel in Copenhagen. Believing that every element was essential for the total effect, Jacobsen paid careful attention to every furnishing in the hotel from the lampshades that hung in the lobby, the ashtrays in which guests stubbed out their cigarettes and the lamps under which they read their newspapers. That is the reason that so many of the Jacobsen products from that time have entered into design history.

In the late 1950s, the architect was commissioned to design the exterior and interiors of the hotel. Jacobsen created the Swan Sofa primarily for use in the suites, lounges and the panoramic Dining Room on the 25th floor of the hotel. The sofa is an elongated version of his Swan Chair, also designed for the hotel, capable of seating two people comfortably. Its shell, a moulded synthetic material covered by a layer of cold foam, elegantly rests on an exposed satin-polished aluminium shaker base. The appeal of the sofa lies in its curves – rather like those of the Egg Chair.

The sofa was in production between 1964 and 1974 and was then reissued by Fritz Hansen in 2000.

☞ **Items to look out for**

The original Swan Sofa produced for 10 years between 1964 and '74 by Fritz Hansen.

Top Tips

A more modern licensed version is available in a host of different fabrics and colours. It retails at upwards of £6,000 (US $9,600).

Websites

Fritz Hansen
www.fritzhansen.com

Also See

■ **Model 3107 (Series 7)**, pages 54–5;
   Egg Chair, pages 64–5
■ **Cutlery**, pages 116–7;
   Cylinda Tea Service, pages 128–9
■ **AJ Light**, pages 144–5

Egg
Nanna Ditzel

Danish designer Nanna Ditzel established a studio with her husband Jørgen in Copenhagen. Her love of nature and interest in new techniques allowed her to create works such as the iconic hanging Egg.

Born in Copenhagen in 1923, Nanna Ditzel trained as a cabinetmaker before attending the School of Arts and Crafts and the Royal Academy of Fine Arts in the city. She set up a studio with her husband Jørgen Ditzel after graduating in furniture design in the mid-1940s.

In the post-war years, Ditzel became well known for experimenting in new techniques and materials. She incorporated fibreglass, wickerwork and foam rubber, among other elements, into her diverse designs, which included objects for the table, textiles and jewellery. She was commissioned by various eminent design manufacturers, including Georg Jensen, Getama and Kvist. Her work garnered various international prizes.

Ditzel and her husband also published the book *Danish Chairs* (1954), which is viewed by many as contributing to the renewal of interest in chair design. Perhaps her most recognized chair is the suspended Egg from the late 1950s. Essentially a hanging armchair, the Egg was produced in a natural woven wicker. It could be suspended from above by a nickel-plated chain or it could hang on a special steel frame. A separate covered cushion came with the chair. Deemed a classic, the Egg is widely viewed as an example of naturalist Scandinavian design at its best.

☞ **Items to look out for**

The original Nanna Ditzel chair can cost upwards of £2,091 (US $3,560).

Top Tips

Many superstores make cheaper copies of the Egg so please check the provenance before investing.

Websites

Nanna Ditzel
www.nanna-ditzel.dk
Pierantonio Bonacina
www.pierantoniobonacina.it

Oxchair
Hans J. Wegner

The beautiful Oxchair is a statement. Strong and bold yet designed with clean, crisp lines, this 1960 Hans J. Wegner design exudes strength and is also very stylish. It is an example of Wegner's belief that furniture can be functional and beautiful.

Hans J. Wegner's chairs helped put mid-20th-century Danish design on the international map and also popularized it, making it available to people who otherwise wouldn't have been able to afford it. Wegner began his career as a cabinetmaker – although he trained to be an architect – and garnered experience working with the influential and much-revered fellow Dane designer Arne Jacobsen before establishing his own office in the early 1940s. He quickly gained a reputation for producing interesting, well-crafted and sometimes irreverent furniture, such as the Valet Chair.

In 1960, Wegner designed the Oxchair, a padded chair covered with oxhide and raised off the floor by chrome-plated steel legs. Its strong and distinctive design immediately won it fans, as did its resemblance to the shape of a bull and – no less importantly – its comfortableness. It was reported to be Wegner's favourite chair. Johannes Hansen originally made the chair but he ceased its production due to technical problems. It was reissued in 1989 by Erik Jørgensen.

To mark the 50th anniversary of the Oxchair, an exclusive limited edition was made in black, natural or burgundy red vegetable-tanned leather. The seats were numbered and came with a special book.

☞ Items to look out for

The original Oxchair is rare and can go for five figures.

The 50th-anniversary limited edition chair is specially numbered and comes with an anniversary book.

🍷 Top Tips

The Oxchair is in demand and even modern versions may entail a six-month wait. The leather version retails at about £5,000 (US $8,000). There is also a footstool, or ottoman, available, priced at £1,250 (US $2,000).

🌐 Websites

Danish Design Store
www.danishdesignstore.com

Erik Jøergensen
www.erik-jøergensen.com

Also See

■ Round Chair, pages 30–1;
Wishbone Chair, pages 42–3;
Teddy Bear Chair (PP19), pages 46–7;
Valet Chair (PP250), pages 48–9

606 Universal Shelving System Dieter Rams

Rams is the master of good design. His 10 commandments detailing what good design is (or isn't) have become the rules by which industrial designers judge themselves. The 606 Universal Shelving System is one of Rams's early products.

Born in Hesse, Germany, in 1932, Dieter Rams studied architecture and interior decorating at Wiesbaden School of Art. In the early 1950s, he began working for acclaimed architect Otto Apel. In 1955, he was recruited by the influential company Braun, which specialized in producing beautifully designed small format electrical goods for the mass market. Rams soon attracted attention with products such as the Phonosuper SK4 record player, which was nicknamed 'Snow White's Coffin', and the T3 portable radio. From the late 1950s, Vitsoe and Zapf began to manufacture Rams's furniture designs and in 1960 he created the 606 Universal Shelving System for them.

Aiming to create designs to fit the changing needs of the early 1960s' domestic market, particularly the youth market, 28-year-old Rams came up with the idea of modular shelving that could be added to and moved around as needed.

Inexpensive but clearly designed along very elegant but functional lines, the 606 is still in production more than 50 years later. To celebrate the 50th anniversary, Vitsoe produced a special version and the Geffrye Museum in London hosted an exhibition dedicated to this classic shelving unit.

☞ Items to look out for
The original Vitsoe 606 from 1960.

❢ Top Tips
A complete unit costs about £285 (US $450).

Websites
Vitsoe
www.vitsoe.com

Also See
▪ **ET44**, pages 130–1

PK24 Chaise Longue (Hammock)
Poul Kjærholm

Danish designer Poul Kjærholm is known for his clean elegant modernist furniture made with an incredible attention to detail as found in the PK24 Chaise Longue, also known as the Hammock, which he designed in 1965.

Trained as a carpenter, Poul Kjærholm graduated from the Copenhagen School of Arts and Crafts in the early 1950s. He loved experimenting with construction materials, particularly steel. He said: 'Steel's constructive potential is not the only thing that interests me; the refraction of light on its surface is an important part of my ... work. I consider steel a material with the same artistic merit as wood and leather.'

The characteristic style of Kjærholm's work – clean and elegant lines and the fine attention to even the smallest detail – was evident at an early stage of his career. He worked at Danish furniture design company Fritz Hansen for a year before collaborating with manufacturer Ejvind Kold Christensen, a working relationship that lasted until Kjærholm's death in 1980. Fritz Hansen still manufactures the designs developed from 1951 to 1967, including the PK24 Chaise Longue, which Kjærholm nicknamed the 'Hammock'.

For the PK24, Kjærholm was influenced by the rococo period and the idea of the French long chair. In the original design, the wicker seat actually has no physical connection with the satin-brushed stainless steel base. These two parts are kept together by gravity and the friction between them.

☞ **Items to look out for**

The PK24 can cost as much as £14,000 (US $22,400).

🕯 **Top Tips**

More modern versions are available in leather or wicker and both come with a headrest.

🖳 **Websites**

Fritz Hansen
www.fritzhansen.com

Ribbon Chair
Pierre Paulin

Featured in the cult British television series *Space 1999*, industrial designer Pierre Paulin's stunningly innovative Ribbon Chair was created in 1966. It won the Chicago Design Award two years later.

French designer Pierre Paulin stated that 'A chair should be more than simply functional. It should be friendly, fun and colourful.' His Ribbon Chair, deemed by many to be one of the most comfortable chairs ever made, is proof that Paulin put his money where his mouth is!

Paulin studied stone carving and clay modelling in Paris, where he began designing furniture for the acclaimed company Thonet. In the late 1950s, he joined Artifort, designing a series of chairs with an inner structure of steel tubing covered in foam and fabric.

The Ribbon Chair was created for Artifort in the mid-1960s. It comprises a tubular steel frame with horizontal springs covered by moulded foam and upholstered in any number of fabrics. The base of the chair is lacquered pressed wood.

Considered by some to be one of the most beautiful chairs in the world, the Ribbon Chair is an acquired taste. Some critics find its strongly contoured and unconventional shape too much to take, but there is method in Paulin's apparent madness. The chair's contoured form is specially designed to enable the user to assume a variety of positions while still being given essential support.

☞ **Items to look out for**

The 1966 model made for Artifort.

One of the Ribbon Chairs featured in *Space 1999*.

Top Tips

Available in many different colours and fabrics the Ribbon Chair costs about £6,500 (US $10,400). A matching Ribbon Ottoman is also available.

Websites

Artifort
www.artifort.com

Bubble Chair
Eero Aarnio

Mixing space-age design with fun, Eero Aarnio's Bubble Chair challenged ideas of what a chair should be and do when it was produced in 1968. Based on Aarnio's earlier Ball Chair, the Bubble Chair is clear like a soap bubble.

The Finnish designer Eero Aarnio is the master of using industrial plastics in modern domestic design.

After establishing his own studio in 1962, Aarnio began to experiment with materials. First came the Ball Chair, a 'room within a room', an iconic chair essentially made of a fibreglass ball that was cut and attached to a metal swivelling base. This chair, also known as the Globe, was upholstered in foam and originally produced in white, red, black and orange. Aarnio, however, wanted to produced a chair with more light. Working on the design, he came up with the Bubble Chair, a chair in which the user could sit cocooned in a sphere while still being aware of the world through its transparent walls.

The designer said: 'The only suitable material is acrylic, which is heated and blown into a shape like a soap bubble. Since I knew that the dome-shaped skylights are made in this way, I contacted the manufacturer and asked if it would be technically possible to blow a bubble that is bigger than a hemisphere. The answer was yes. I had a steel ring made, the bubble was blown and cushions were added and the chair was ready. And, again, the name was obvious: BUBBLE.'

☞ **Items to look out for**

The Bubble Chair can cost upwards of £5,000 (US $8,000).

🍴 **Top Tips**

Nanna Ditzel's Egg is often confused with the Bubble Chair. The Egg is an earlier design.

There are very many fakes on the market. Look carefully at the provenance of the chair.

[www] **Websites**

Eero Aarnio
www.eero-aarnio.com

Panton Stacking Chair
Verner Panton

Stylish, sexy and fun, the Panton Stacking Chair made its first appearance in 1967. Now instantly recognizable, the chair is probably the most famous of Panton's many iconic designs.

Remembered for the use of psychedelic colours, space-age design and modern materials in his many products, Verner Panton designed the Panton Stacking Chair in 1960, but it had to wait seven years before going into production.

The chair made its first appearance in 1967 in the Danish design magazine *Mobilia* and immediately created a huge storm. Its sleek, colourful curved design and the groundbreaking idea of a cantilever chair made from one continuous piece of plastic immediately grabbed the imagination of the critics and popular audiences alike.

Panton found support from Willi Fehlbaum, founder of German furniture design company Vitra. With the help of company technicians, Panton and Fehlbaum developed the chair from its original 1960 concept to one better suited to a mass-market audience. The chair was first produced in polyester resin reinforced with fibreglass and then later in polyurethane rigid foam. Recent developments in plastics technology have made it possible to produce much cheaper versions. The Panton Stacking Chair currently produced by Vitra is made from rigid expanded polypropylene with a lacquered surface.

☞ **Items to look out for**

The original chairs made of polyester resin reinforced with fibreglass.

💡 **Top Tips**

The Panton Stacking Chair retails from £834 (US $1,335). It is made from rigid expanded plastic with a lacquered surface. A cheaper version also exists made of lower-grade plastic.

🌐 **Websites**

Skandium
www.skandium.com
Vitra
www.vitra.com

Also See

■ Moon Lamp, pages 152–3;
FlowerPot, pages 160–1;
VP Globe, pages 162–3;
Spiral Triple SP3, pages 164–5

Soft Pad Chair
Charles and Ray Eames

Fearlessly adventurous, husband-and-wife team Charles and Ray Eames pushed the boundaries of design by creating some of the most iconic yet practical interior designs. The Soft Pad Chair from the late 1960s is among them.

The association between Charles and Ray Eames and Herman Miller proved a commercial, lucrative and innovative success. Between them, they created some of the best examples of modernist furniture of the 20th century and their work is featured in pretty much every major design museum around the world. Hugely popular with collectors, their products are also among the most copied. Originals require quite a major investment by a collector and licensed Herman Miller products are still available but at a high cost.

The Soft Pad Chair came about through the creation of the Eameses' earlier Aluminium Chair. Architect, designer and friend Eero Saarinen asked the pair to design a high-quality outdoor chair for the industrialist J. Irwin Miller's home. The result was a chair made from cast aluminium with an innovative seat-back suspension. It was a major departure from the concept of the chair as a solid shell. In 1958, Herman Miller began manufacturing the Aluminium Chair. Eleven years later, the Eameses extended the range by adding plush cushions to the frame. The Soft Pad Chair, as it is now known, has become very popular in offices. Today, it is made of 60 percent recycled materials and 90 percent of the chair is recyclable.

☞ Items to look out for

The original 1969 model.

💡 Top Tips

It is possible to buy a modern version of the Soft Pad from Herman Miller and Vitra for about £2,500 (US $4,000) without arms (known as the Side Chair). Arms can be included for an additional £155 (US $250).

🖳 Websites

Herman Miller
www.hermanmiller.com

Vitra
www.vitra.com

Also See

■ LCW (Lounge Chair Wood), pages 26–7;
   La Chaise, pages 36–7;
   LAR, DAR and RAR, pages 38–9;
   ESU Bookshelf, pages 44–5;
   Model 670 and Model 671 (Lounge Chair and Ottoman), pages 60–1

■ Hang-It-All, pages 108–9

S Chair
Tom Dixon

A chair that pays more than a nod to Verner Panton's classic Stacking Chair, British designer Tom Dixon's S Chair uses natural materials to create a product that is less industrial and more organic.

Self-taught British designer Tom Dixon experiments with texture and materials to create very interesting and innovative work. Pieces of his furniture such as the S Chair, released in 1991, showcase Dixon's distinctive style, as well as referencing outside influences. The cantilevered structure of early Marcel Breuer chairs, the curves of the Panton Stacking Chair and even African traditional craftwork are all evident in the design of Dixon's S Chair.

Dixon, who handcrafted the chair, experimented with many different materials, including rubber and paper, before settling on using two types of covering: gnarled woven marsh straw and wicker. The frame is made of dark lacquered metal and is stabilized by a circular base. The uneven surface gives the chair an organic urban chic that is missing in the plastic chairs of Pop Art designers such as Panton.

The S Chair appealed to a specific design market, as catered to by Italian furniture manufacturer Cappellini, which eventually put the chair into mass production. Dixon's original wicker and marsh-straw designs are still produced today, as are versions with a fixed cover in various coloured fabrics and materials, including black-and-white pony leather.

☞ Items to look out for

The original S Chair was made in woven marsh straw or wicker. Later models have different coverings.

♦ Top Tips

There are limited-edition versions made by Cappellini such as the 2003 version, which uses a deconstruction of the company's trademark to decorate the chair.

 Websites

Cappellini
www.cappellini.it
Tom Dixon
www.tomdixon.net

Also See

■ **Panton Stacking Chair**, pages 80–1

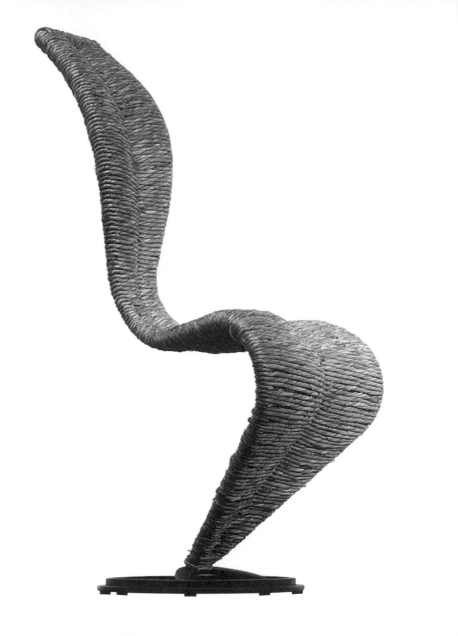

Balzac Armchair and Ottoman Matthew Hilton

When British designer Matthew Hilton created the Balzac Armchair and Ottoman for the design retailer SCP in 1991, they were an instant success. Since then, Hilton has designed many other ranges of furniture.

British designer Matthew Hilton was born in Hastings, Sussex, in 1957. He studied furniture design at Kingston Polytechnic in the 1970s and after graduating began designing and manufacturing low-tech cast metal objects. His products achieved some recognition when British fashion retailer Paul Smith and French company Joseph Pour La Maison sold them in their London showrooms.

In the mid-1980s, Hilton established his own self-named design company and began a collaboration with manufacturer and cutting-edge British retailer SCP. Now Based in Shoreditch, East London, SCP released their first Hilton-designed pieces, the Balzac Armchair and Ottoman, in 1991.

The Balzac has a solid beech frame with steel springs and elasticated webbing, covered in multi-density foam with a feather cushion and American oak legs. Full of comfortable curves and encased in soft aniline leather, the Balzac has become a modern design classic, suitable for use in homes, bars and clubs.

The Balzac Armchair helped establish Matthew Hilton's reputation as an influential designer. He has since expanded the range to include the Balzac Ottoman and Two- and Three-Seater Sofas.

Items to look out for

The original Balzac Armchair and Ottoman retail at about £3,030 (US $4,850).

Top Tips

The Balzac Armchair can be bought separately at £2,798 (US $4,480).

It is possible to buy Two- and Three-Seater Balzac Sofas.

Websites

Heal's
www.heals.co.uk

SCP
www.scp.co.uk

Charles Sofa
Antonio Citterio

A leading Italian designer, Antonio Citterio is known for his beautiful yet functional and comfortable designs. The Charles Sofa is one of his most famous pieces of furniture.

Born in Italy in 1950, Citterio studied architecture at the University of Milan and opened his own studio in 1972. Over the years, Citterio has had long and fruitful collaborations with many internationally respected and innovative design companies, including B&B Italia, Flos, Kartell, Arclinea and Vitra. In 1999, he established Antonio Citterio and Partners, which is a multidisciplinary architecture and design studio. He has won several prestigious prizes for his designs, including the Compasso d'Oro in 1987 and 1995. His work is also part of the permanent collection at the Museum of Modern Art (MoMA) in New York.

The Charles Sofa is probably one of Citterio's best known designs. Originally manufactured in 1996 by B&B Italia, it soon became recognized for its elegant simplicity. Die-cast inverted L-shaped aluminium feet, a long single-cushioned seat and free floating cushions along the back made the Charles Sofa stylish, functional and also comfortable. Immediately popular with audiences, the Charles Sofa was a success. In 2003, Citterio revisited his design and a revised larger model was released, with added attention to comfort. The following year, the Charles Bed was added to the collection.

☞ **Items to look out for**

The Charles Sofa retails at more than £3,000 (US $4,800).

🍷 **Top Tips**

There are several modular versions of the sofa. The Charles is recognizable from inverted L-shaped aluminium feet.

🖳 **Websites**

B&B Italia
www.bebitalia.com

Loop Table
Barber Osgerby

Barber Osgerby is the love child of British designers Edward Barber and Jay Osgerby. The Loop Table was their first collaboration under this name. It is a much desired item of furniture and is a product that exudes simple elegance.

After graduating from the Royal College of Art in London with master degrees in architecture and design, Edward Barber and Jay Osgerby established their first studio in Trellick Tower in West London. In 1997, they created the Loop Table for Isokon Plus.

The partners have, since the inception of their company, gained a solid reputation for producing beautifully crafted work across a range of areas, from the interior design of classic bar–restaurants such as the former Pharmacy in Notting Hill Gate to working with Murano-based glass makers Venini to produce a series of large-scale limited-edition vases.

The Loop Table is the foundation on which all this success is built. Brilliant in its simplicity, it was originally conceived as part of an outfit for a restaurant but proved too expensive to produce. It gathered dust for almost two years before Isokon took it on. It was produced by Cappellini in Italy. Today, it sits in the permanent collections of New York's Museum of Modern Art (MoMA) and London's Victoria and Albert Museum (V&A). Literally made of a loop of laminated wood, with the lower half forming a shelf, the table became, according to the British newspaper the *Observer*: 'a super iconic example of 90s design'.

☞ **Items to look out for**

The Loop is available in birch, oak and walnut.

💡 **Top Tips**

The birch version is the cheapest at £1,100 (US $1,760); oak and walnut Loop Tables cost £1,190 (US $1,900) each.

It is now possible to buy a Loop Shelf to match the table. This retails at £230 (US $370) for the birch version and £250 (US $400) for the oak and walnut pieces.

🌐 **Websites**

Isokon Plus
www.isokonplus.com

Also See

■ **Isokon Long Chair**, pages 22–3; **Isokon Penguin Donkey**, pages 24–5

Low Pad
Jasper Morrison

English designer Jasper Morrison is renowned for his collaborations with various international companies. His stylishly comfortable Low Pad was produced by Cappellini in Italy and is a modern-day classic chair.

Born in London in 1959, Jasper Morrison attended Kingston Polytechnic Design School and the Royal College of Art in London before winning a scholarship to study at Berlin's HdK (now Berlin University of the Arts). In the mid-1980s, Morrison set up a design office in London, where he began to work on various high-profile projects, such as the Reuters News Centre installation for the Documenta 8 exhibition in Kassel, Germany.

Morrison started to attract attention when he collaborated with several leading international companies, including the East London-based design company SCP, the office-furniture company Vitra and the Italian furniture producer Cappellini. For Cappellini, he co-organized Progetto Oggetto, a collection of household objects devised with a group of young European designers. His chair the Low Pad, designed in 1999, was also produced by Cappellini.

The Low Pad combines style and comfort with sleek design. Essentially an armchair that can exist with or without arms, it is made with a plywood and multi-density polyurethane foam seat. The chair can be covered in fabric or leather and is suitable for office use or in a design-conscious home. The chair's legs are made of satined stainless steel and have rubber feet.

☞ **Items to look out for**

The Low Pad retails at about £835 (US $1,335).

🍸 **Top Tips**

The Low Pad is available with or without arms and can be covered in fabric or leather.

🔲 **Websites**

Cappellini
www.cappellini.com

Jasper Morrison Products
www.jaspermorrison.com

Tea Service
Wilhelm Wagenfeld

Wagenfeld designed the glass tea service for which he has become famous for Jenaer Glaswerk in the early 1930s. It sits in the permanent collections of several museums, including the Museum of Modern Art (MoMA) in New York.

German industrial designer and printmaker Wilhelm Wagenfeld joined the Bauhaus workshop in the 1920s. He became one of Germany's leading industrial designers during the 1930s.

Erich Schott, the principal of Jenaer Glaswerk, commissioned the designer to develop heat-resistant glassware. Schott wanted a range of good-looking ware that could be used both in the kitchen and at the table. The streamlined, pure lines of the Tea Service, which Wagenfeld designed in the early 1930s, were well received. The service featured a cream jug, sugar bowl, plates, a tray and teacups and saucers (in two sizes); its most striking item was the teapot (in three sizes), with a central infuser–strainer (see opposite).

Although Schott wanted the designer's name to appear on the service, Wagenfeld later said: 'Practical and rational considerations spoke against this idea. I recommended eliminating even the family name of the enterprise in a new trademark design. The consumer should remember merely the name of the place from where the glass came. This would increase his appreciation of the product itself.' Wagenfeld believed that industrial products were the collective expression of a number of individuals, working together.

☞ Items to look out for

The 1930s' Tea Service. A complete service can be priced between £750 and £2,190 (US $1,200–3,500) at auction.

Wagenfeld's c.1924 Bauhaus Lamp.

♦ Top Tips

Look for the old 1930s' maker's mark.

▭ Websites

Museum of Modern Art
www.moma.org

Tea Trolley 901
Alvar Aalto

Considered one of the most influential designers of the 20th century, Alvar Aalto had a softer approach to modernist design that brought him great popularity. Items such as the Tea Trolley 901 were made for his company, Artek, in the 1930s.

Finnish architect and designer Alvar Aalto believed that the people buying his pieces had the right to have something that was beautiful and stylish but also comfortable in their households. He invented new processes to mould plywood and bond veneers, and began experimenting with laminated birch furniture in 1927 after meeting Otto Korhonen of the Oy Huonekalu-ja factory.

The demand for Aalto's furniture increased in the 1930s and by 1935 he had set up a company, Artek, with his wife to commercially mass produce his designs.

Aalto designed the birch-wood Tea Trolley 901 in 1936. It debuted at the at the Paris Exposition in 1937. He conceived the trolley for residential use, placing it in the living room of Villa Mairea, a guest house he designed in the late 1930s in Noormarkku, Finland. The trolley is based on an earlier serving cart produced in 1933 for the Paimio (TB) Sanatorium, for which Aalto had also developed his famous 41 Paimio Chair.

The large white wheels of the trolley had black rubber treads so as not to damage the floor and the trolley shelf and top had a black linoleum or white laminate veneer. From its inception, the trolley was very popular. It remains a much sought-after item today.

🖙 **Items to look out for**

The original Tea Trolley was made from birch wood topped by white laminate or black linoleum.

💡 **Top Tips**

Artek still produces the trolley, which ships fully assembled. It can be found for about £1,549 (US $2,480).

🖵 **Websites**

Artek
www.artek.fi
The Conran Shop
www.conranshop.co.uk

Also See

■ **41 Paimio**, pages 20–1
■ **Savoy Vase**, pages 172–3

Sunburst Clock
George Nelson

Along with Ray and Charles Eames, George Nelson was considered one of the leading exponents of modernism in the United States. His iconic 1949 Sunburst Clock is still considered a design classic.

George Nelson described his creative impulses as a series of 'zaps', which he explained as 'when the solitary individual finds he is connected with a reality he never dreamed of'. Over the five decades of his career, Nelson had some impressive zaps. His ideas influenced the development of 20th-century design through concepts such as the downtown pedestrian mall, Storagewall, the first modular storage system and the iconic Marshmallow Sofa. However, most people know Nelson best through his 1949 Sunburst Clock.

An article on the Storagewall in 1945 first brought Nelson to the attention of D.J. De Pree at Herman Miller, a major manufacturer of office furniture and equipment. Through his company George Nelson and Associates, Nelson enjoyed a long collaboration with Herman Miller, for whom he produced some of his most influential work. Nelson designed clocks for Herman Miller from 1947 onwards. Over the years, he produced more than 150 designs, of which the Sunburst Clock is one of his most recognizable. The original models were given serial numbers; the Ball Clock was known as Clock 4755 and the Sunburst as Clock 2202. Made in enamelled metal, 47cm (18.5in) across, the originals bear the manufacturer's stamp and model number.

Items to look out for

If you're buying a licensed product, look for the original stamp.

Top Tips

Watch out for more modern versions of the clock, which can retail at as little as £20 (US $30).

Websites

Heal's
www.heals.co.uk
Vitra
www.vitra.com/en-gb

Also See

■ **Marshmallow Sofa**, pages 62–3

Europiccola
La Pavoni

Loved by coffee connoisseurs, the lever machine Europiccola is an aspirational product seen in the very best houses around the world. It is an Italian design classic.

Designed and manufactured by the Milan-based company La Pavoni, the Europiccola is considered one of the finest coffee machines in the world.

La Pavoni was founded in Milan in 1905 by Desiderio Pavoni, whose first invention was an espresso coffee machine for a bar called Ideale. The machine soon became popular, helping to promote the fashion of drinking Italian-style espresso coffee at a bar. However, it sometimes resulted in a slightly sour, burnt taste caused by steam – in addition to water – being released through the coffee. In 1948, a new mechanism allowed the water to be heated under pressure, before being filtered through the coffee by way of a piston operated by a spring at 10 bars pressure. This innovation resulted in very good coffee without that pervading burnt taste.

La Pavoni released their classic lever machine, the Europiccola, in 1950. Largely constructed of cast brass, the machine was designed to last while being stylish and efficient. It was revolutionary in that the lever allowed the user to vary the speed at which the water passed through the coffee, ensuring that it can be made exactly to his or her specific taste. This feature has resulted in the Europiccola being much desired by coffee drinkers around the world.

Items to look out for

The Europiccola.

Top Tips

Shop around. While the Europiccola is expensive at about £560 (US $900), it is possible to buy the machine for as little as £370 (US $590) on the internet.

Websites

La Pavoni
www.lapavoni.it

Wooden Monkey
Kay Bojesen

It may seem odd to include a wooden toy in a book on collectables, but Danish designer Kay Bojesen's Wooden Monkey remains iconic almost five decades after its original release.

Although Kay Bojesen was a silversmith, winning a prize in Milan for his Grand Prix cutlery in 1951, it is for his wooden toys that he is probably best known. Bojesen started as the celebrated Georg Jensen's apprentice and worked in Germany, France and Copenhagen. In the 1930s, he began experimenting with wood. He created the Wooden Monkey in 1951.

Using extraordinary craftsmanship, Bojesen made his animal in unvarnished teak and limba wood. The limbs are jointed at the shoulders, wrists, hips and ankles, and are movable. The monkey's head can swivel too. A long curved section of pale limba wood forms the upper half of the monkey's face, which has an impish expression. Its light-coloured potbelly has an indented navel. The toy has clean lines and a simplicity of design that made it an immediate success. It was so popular in the early 1950s that London's Victoria and Albert Museum (V&A) exhibited it. Bojesen later increased his wooden toy stable, designing a Wooden Elephant and Bear to join his Monkey.

In 1990, Rosendahl Copenhagen bought the rights to Bojesen's Wooden Monkey, along with those to all of his other products. To this day, the Wooden Monkey remains a very popular design item.

☞ **Items to look out for**

The Rosendahl Monkey: a small monkey 20cm (8in) retails at about £138 (US $200); the larger version 60cm (24in) costs between £500 and £1,425 (US $800–2,280).

Originals can go for about £10,000 (US $16,000).

The Rosendahl Elephant, Bear, Wooden Horse and Guardsmen.

💡 **Top Tips**

The Wooden Monkey's limbs and head are movable.

🖥 **Websites**

Rosendahl Copenhagen
www.rosendahl.com

Also See

◼ **Teak Bowl,** pages 104–5

Teak Bowl
Finn Juhl

Celebrated Danish architect and designer Finn Juhl became famous for his beautiful furniture through models such as the Chieftain Chair and NV-45 but he also created a range of lovely housewares, including the 1951 Teak Bowl.

In the 1940s, Finn Juhl's designs helped regenerate Danish furniture design. His later designs were more specifically aimed at the mass market and providing well-designed everyday goods at reasonable prices.

Although Juhl was successful, his peers such as Hans J. Wegner were better respected in his native country. His work, however, began to be known in the United States after appearing in *Interiors* magazine towards the end of the 1940s. Juhl's work was also featured in the Good Design Exhibition in Chicago in 1951.

Influenced by surrealists such as Jean Arp and Joan Miró, the designer applied these masters' use of shapes and curves that occur in nature – biomorphism – to help explore the sculptural possibilities of wooden furniture, as seen in his Teak Bowl from the early 1950s. A durable hardwood, teak is often associated with Scandinavian furniture. It combines lightness with durability and its natural colour and oil give items a softness and sheen, suitable for the modernists' adherence to truth and functionality in their design.

Finn Juhl designed several bowls in the 1950s, including the tiny Teak Footed Bowl and the bowl featured opposite. They were made by master lathe operator Magne Monsen at Kay Bojesen's workshop.

☞ **Items to look out for**

Also of interest is the tiny but rare Teak Footed Bowl from this period. It is 7.5cm (3in) high and 23.5cm (9.25in) wide.

💡 **Top Tips**

The original bowl is 13.5x26.5x29.5cm (5.3x10.4x11.6in). It is stamped with 'Finn Juhl/Kay Bojesen, Denmark. Copyright Finn Juhl Design'. It is much sought after and even on sites like eBay can command more than £3,750 (US $6,000).

🖳 **Websites**

Dansk Møbelkunst
www.dmk.dk

One Collection: The House of Finn Juhl
www.onecollection.com

Also See

◼ **NV-45**, pages 28–9;
   Chieftain Chair, pages 40–1
◼ **Wooden Monkey**, pages 102–3

Krenit Bowl
Herbert Krenchel

In 1953, Danish civil engineer and materials researcher Herbert Krenchel designed the Krenit Bowl. It won the gold medal for design at the Milan Triennials in 1954.

Krenchel designed the Krenit Range for the Danish manufacturer Torben Ørskov. The idea was to create something simple, classic and functional that could be used in the kitchen, at the dining table or for decoration elsewhere in the home. After much experimentation, Krenchel devised a method that made it possible to produce the bowls from millimetre-thick steel plate. Machine-pressed cold, the resulting vessels tapered to a paper-thin lip and combined cool matt black exteriors with vibrantly coloured enamel-coated interiors. The bowls were acid resistant and could be put directly into fire. The name 'Krenit' derives from Krenchel's own name and eternit, the fibre cement used in coating the bowls' exterior. At the time, they were groundbreaking in terms of mass-produced wares. Manufacture of the bowls ran between 1953 and 1966, during which time more than one million units were sold.

In addition to the bowls, which were produced in a variety of sizes, the Krenit Range included a jug, plates and salad servers. In 2009, Danish company Normann Copenhagen relaunched the Krenit Bowl, with white, red, lime, and turquoise interiors. The original Krenit Series can be seen in design museums around the world; the bowl is highly collectable.

Items to look out for

Original Krenit Bowls can go for £90 to £125 (US $145–200).

A 30cm (12in) Normann new range Krenit Salad Bowl retails at about £22 (US $35).

Top Tips

The Normann Copenhagen Krenit Bowls are usually produced in a more limited range of colours than the 1950s and '60s originals. They are also shallower than the originals. Salad bowls retail at about £24 (US $38).

The 'badekaret' sized bowl (literally 'bath tub') is a newly produced Normann bowl. The original Krenit Bowls were never this size.

Websites

Normann Copenhagen
www.shop.normann-copenhagen.com

Hang-It-All
Charles and Ray Eames

Esteemed designers Charles and Ray Eames created a line of products aimed at children, including the 1953 Hang-It-All for Tigrett Enterprises Playhouse Division. Today, it can often be seen in design-conscious homes.

Husband-and-wife team Charles and Ray Eames are probably among the most recognized designers of the mid-20th century. The Eameses influenced later furniture design and were supporters of the modernist ideal that industry and art could be combined. The couple met at the Cranbrook Academy of Art, in Michigan, where they counted among their friends other leading modernists such as Finnish–American architect Eero Saarinen. Shortly after their marriage in 1941, they moved to Los Angeles, where they began to design in earnest. There, they produced some of the work for which they would become best known, such as the LCW (Lounge Chair Wood).

In the 1950s, the Eameses also produced goods for Tigrett Enterprises, including the Hang-It-All. Designed to encourage children to hang up their clothes, it was made of a white plastic-coated steel-wire frame decorated with brightly coloured gloss-painted wooden balls. Almost too beautiful to cover up, the Hang-It-All was fun, exuberant and seemed almost too simple a design. To achieve the right effect, the Eameses utilized the mass-production techniques for welding wires that they had developed for their wire-base tables and wire chairs.

Items to look out for

The 1953 item in its original box with the manufacturer's shipping label, featuring a return address of 'The Playhouse' in Jackson, Tennessee, the headquarters of Tigrett.

Top Tips

Vitra produces a modern version of Hang-It-All for about £182 (US $290).

Websites

Dansk Møbelkunst
www.dmk.dk
Herman Miller
www.hermanmiller.com
Vitra
www.vitra.com

Also See

LCW (Lounge Chair Wood), pages 26–7; DAR, RAR and LAR, pages 38–9; ESU Bookshelf, pages 44–5; Model 670 and 671 (Lounge Chair and Ottoman), pages 60–1

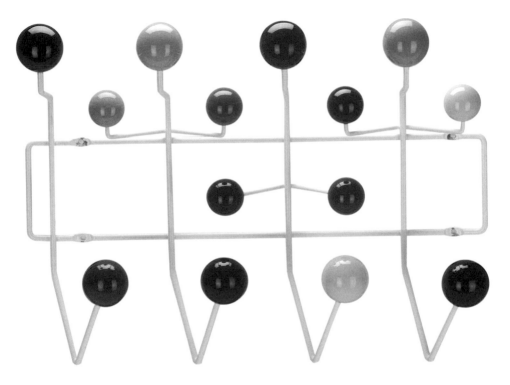

Ericofon
Blomberg/Lysell/Gösta Thames

Also known as the Cobra (Kobra) and Ericafon, the Swedish Ericofon was named one of the best industrial designs of the 20th century by the Museum of Modern Art (MoMA) in New York. It was discontinued in the 1970s but reissued again in 2001.

The post-war period brought great technical and technological innovation and exciting opportunities to designers and manufacturers. They were now able to apply methods or use materials previously only available in industrial and military spheres for domestic wares. Consumers wanted well-designed products that were inexpensive, easy to use and modern. New, more versatile plastics allowed this innovation to occur. This is was particularly evident in the creation of the Ericofon by the Swedish company Ericsson that used the thermoplastic acrylonitrile butadiene styrene (ABS), which was impact resistant and could be made in any colour as opposed to Bakelite's basic black.

In 1949, Ericsson put together a design team, headed by H. Gösta Thames, to develop a stylish, small and lightweight phone for the industrial market. Based on an earlier prototype by Hugo Blomberg and Ralph Lysell from 1941, the snake-shaped Ericofon went into production in 1954. Revolutionary, it consisted of a single handset that housed the dial, receiver and speaker.

The Ericofon was released in Europe and Australia. The Bell Company, who held the US monopoly, was initially resistant to market a foreign phone. After it relented, the Ericofon was a huge success in the 1960s.

☞ Items to look out for

The original US model from the 1960s, available in 18 colours, including Taj Mahal (white) and Chartreuse (pale green).

Model 700 is the 1976 version introduced by Ericsson to celebrate its centenary and was made only in Sweden.

☀ Top Tips

The Ericsson model number started with DBJ500; the British model had the number 600 and US company North Electric used 52 for its rotary version. They can retail at up to £120 (US $190).

The rotary dial is hidden in the base. After 1967, the dial was replaced with buttons.

When buying also look for items listed as Cobrafons, Ericafons or Kobratons.

▨ Websites

The History of Ericsson
www.ericssonhistory.com

Flensted Mobile
Christian and Grethe Flensted

Since 1954, when Christian and Grethe Flensted created their first mobile to celebrate the baptism of their daughter Mette, Flensted Mobiles have been extremely popular with children and adults alike.

In 1954, Christian and Grethe Flensted made their first mobile, Lucky Storks (still in production today, over 50 years later), to celebrate their daughter Mette's birth. Created so that the storks are in constant motion, the mobile was an almost instant success. Denmark has a tradition of mobile making but the Flensted design was significant as it marked a change in the mobile's use, making it a moving work of art for the home and not just something to hang over a crib.

Also known as the 'Uromager', which roughly translates as 'a maker of mischievous things that are always on the move', Christian Flensted gave up his job in 1956 to concentrate on making mobiles. The Flensteds moved (within Denmark) from Aalborg to Tommerup, on the island of Funen, where they expanded their range of mobiles. Within 15 years, the company was so successful that the Flensteds had to move to a larger building, an old school near Brenderup on Funen.

Flensted employees work from home assembling the mobiles, thus saving what the company estimates is more than 10 tonnes (9.8 tons) of fuel every year. Today, the Flensteds' son Ole and his wife Aase run the company. Among the many mobiles the Flensteds produce is the Happy Whales (see opposite).

☞ **Items to look out for**

The original 1954 model of Lucky Storks. Although the model is still in production the original mobile is collectable.

🔗 **Top Tips**

The model Flowing Rhythm is very iconic as it was featured in the film *Who's Afraid of Virginia Woolf?* (1966), starring the late Richard Burton and Elizabeth Taylor.

www **Websites**

Flensted Mobiles
www.flensted-mobiles.com

Teapot
Sori Yanagi

Sori Yanagi is one of the most influential designers of post-war Japan. His lovely Butterfly Stool and Elephant Stool, both from *c.*1956, and Teapot are among many of his iconic pieces.

The son of Soetsu Yanagi, who was a leading figure in the Japanese Folk Arts and Craft Movement, Sori Sanagi was born in Tokyo in 1915. After attending art school, Yanagi gained vital experience from 1940 to 1942 working in the Japanese offices of the French designer Charlotte Perriand, who was arts and craft adviser to the Japanese Board of Trade at the time. Perriand famously collaborated with Le Corbusier on several award-winning designs (see Furniture section).

Yanagi established an industrial design institute in 1952, where he began to produce the work for which he is best known. His work mixes Japanese simplicity and purity with western design and manufacturing processes. It is this combination that makes his designs so appealing to collectors.

In 1956, Yanagi designed the porcelain Teapot, which is both functional and aesthetically pleasing. It has a bamboo handle and dimensions of 12.7x 15.25cm (6x5in). In 1957, Yanagi won the gold award for his Butterfly Stool at 11th Milan Triennials. He has also designed lighting, glass and children's toys. In addition, his reach stretches to underground station, car and motorbike design. In 1977, Yanagi became director of the Japanese Folk Art Museum in Tokyo.

Items to look out for

The Teapot costs about £125 (US $200) and comes with a matching creamer and cup.

Top Tips

Not to be confused with the semi-glazed ceramics he produced, which are very beautiful.

Look out for his stainless steel Kitchen Tool Range, including a ladle and fish slice.

Websites

Gateway Japan
www.gatewayjapan.dk

Also See

■ Butterfly Stool, pages 52–3

Cutlery
Arne Jacobsen

Designed in 1957 for the restaurant of the SAS Royal Hotel in Copenhagen, Arne Jacobsen's beautiful cutlery set is masterful in its simplicity and elegance, and typifies the designer's work.

Born in 1902 in Copenhagen, Arne Jacobsen studied architecture. In 1925, while still a student, he travelled to the International Exhibition of Modern Design in Paris and was impressed by L'Esprit Nouveau Pavilion, a temporary building designed by Swiss/French architect Le Corbusier. He also came to admire the Bauhaus group, headed by Walter Gropius, and became increasingly interested in the work of Charles and Ray Eames in the post-war period.

Jacobsen believed that every element of design from 'the spoon to the city' was important. This versatile designer later had the opportunity to explore his guiding principle when he was commissioned to design every element of the SAS Royal Hotel in Copenhagen, from the building itself to its furniture and the stainless steel cutlery used by the guests in the restaurant.

A statement in minimalism, each piece of Jacobsen's cutlery is beautifully crafted – from the scalpel-shaped knives to the elongated forks and spoons, and the offset handles of the soup spoons. This cutlery was later made famous when US film director Stanley Kubrick used it in the iconic *2001: A Space Odyssey*. Today, the silver manufacturer Georg Jensen makes Jacobsen's cutlery in the best-quality steel available.

Items to look out for

The **26-piece original 1950s' set** sells for more than £1,250 (US $2,000).

Top Tips

Today, **Georg Jensen** manufactures the Arne Jacobsen set. A 24-piece service retails at £272 (US $435).

Websites

Georg Jensen
www.georgjensenstore.com

Also See

- **Model 3107 (Series 7)**, pages 54–5;
  Egg Chair, pages 64–5;
  Swan Sofa, pages 66–7
- **Cylinda Tea Service**, pages 128–9
- **AJ Light**, pages 144–5

Wall Clock 32/0389
Max Bill

Max Bill was influenced by the Bauhaus functionalist approach to design. After turning his hand to industrial design, he created the 1957 aluminium Wall Clock 32/0389, which was produced by Junghans. It has a purity and classic simplicity.

Max Bill trained as a silversmith in Zurich in the 1920s, before studying art at Bauhaus in Dessau, where he was taught by artists Josef Albers, Wassily Kandinsky and Paul Klee, among others. In 1929, Bill returned to Zurich, where he worked as an architect, painter, graphic artist, sculptor and industrial designer.

In 1932, Bill joined a group of Paris-based artists known as the Abstraction-Création. He held his first exhibition in Paris in the following year. He also became friends with artists Piet Mondrian and Auguste Herbin. By 1936, he had developed the Principles of Concrete Art, based on the ideas of Dutch artist Theo van Doesburg.

For most people, Max Bill's name instantly conjures up his 1957 iconic Wall Clock 32/0389. Today, it sits in various museum collections around the world, including the Museum of Modern Art (MoMA) in New York. Its almost austere purity and simplicity of design makes the clock a design classic. Originally chrome plated and painted metal, and measuring 6cm (2.4in) in depth and 32.4cm (12.75in) in diameter, the Wall Clock 32/0389 was produced by Gebrüder Junghans AG, based in Schramberg, Germany.

The Wall Clock is still in production today but has an updated movement system.

Items to look out for

Max Bill also designed the ATO-MAT Clock, a ceramic clock with timer. This timepiece can be found for about £450 (US $725).

Top Tips

A newer version of the clock is available in modern materials with an updated movement system. It retails at about £270 (US $430).

Websites

Junghans
www.junghans.de
Max Bill
www.maxbill-watches-clocks-usa.com

Sarpaneva Casserole
Timo Sarpaneva

A versatile designer, happy working in different materials, Timo Sarpaneva was one of FInland's leading artists. His ability to make everyday objects, such as a casserole pot, beautiful have made him popular with modern audiences.

An award-winning designer, Timo Sarpaneva was one of several luminaries whose genius helped introduce Finnish design to an international audience. A master of glass, porcelain, cast iron, graphic art and textiles, Sarpaneva created some of the most iconic and lovely domestic objects of the 20th century. He is also responsible for the Finnish design company Iittala's current trademark, which was developed for his glass collection I-linja (I-line) in 1956. His work, for which he won many awards, can be seen in museum collections around the world.

The Sarpaneva Casserole, created in 1959 and issued by Finnish company Rosenlew, has become, over the years, an iconic piece of design. Made to have many purposes and to be used on a stove, in an oven, on the table and even possibly in the fridge, it is a lovely piece of design. The casserole is a much appreciated and collected piece of work – so much so that it received the distinction of appearing on a Finnish postage stamp!

Sarpaneva drew inspiration from his blacksmith grandfather and made the casserole from cast iron. The casserole has a lovely curved teak handle that allows it to be carried with one hand and can also be cleverly inserted into the lid to open it.

Items to look out for

The original casserole was made of cast iron and teak. It is highly collectable and can cost from £350 (US $560).

Top Tips

Today back in production, the Sarpaneva Casserole is available for about £169 (US $270) from Iittala.

Websites

Iittala
www.iittala.com

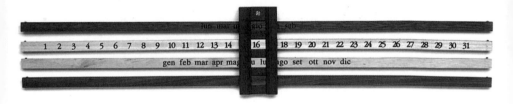

Calendario Bilancia
Enzo Mari

Enzo Mari's classic Calendario Bilancia (Balancing Wall Calendar) is a sculptural as well as practical object. Its mixture of woods is visually interesting and its clever artistry also makes it a balanced but intelligent piece of design.

Designer Enzo Mari was born in Novara, Italy, in 1932. Known as an intellectual designer, who carefully thinks about how his products will look and work in practice, Mari has influenced many younger designers.

In the 1950s, Mari opened a design studio in Milan. Interested in experimenting with systems of design methodology and linear elements and planes, he collaborated with the Italian plastics manufacturer Danese, for whom he created a series of goods aimed at the mass market. One of his first projects, 16 Animali (16 Animals) was a wooden puzzle in which animal shapes such as a snake, giraffe and hippo can be arranged to make a rectangle.

Among young collectors, however, it is the Calendario Bilancia (Balancing Wall Calendar) for which Mari is perhaps best known. Designed in c.1954, it consists of a central block with three horizontal strips of different and contrasting woods, which have the days, numbers and months printed on them using silk-screen methods. A fourth strip of timber acts as a counterbalance. Mari used the woods walnut, ramin, steamed beech and maple in the calendar. The manual balance was criticized by some people but most fans admire the simplicity and elegance of Mari's classic design.

Items to look out for

An original Calendario Bilancia.

Top Tips

More modern versions are available from Danese Milano from £64 (US $102).

Websites

Retro To Go
www.retrotogo.com

The Lollipop Shoppe
www.lollipopshoppe.co.uk

Congo Ice Bucket
Jens Quistgaard

Danish industrial designer Jens Quistgaard's work has become very desirable in recent years. The elegance and practical design of such items as the Congo Ice Bucket make them staple goods in designer homes.

Many people know Quistgaard's designs from his stunningly coloured Kobenstyle enamelled steel cookware created for the company Dansk, founded by US entrepreneur Ted Nierenberg. Quistgaard designed for Dansk from its inception in the 1950s until the 1980s. The clean lines of his household pieces, in particular, helped promote Scandinavian design around the world, especially in America.

Born in 1919 in Denmark, Quistgaard came from an artistic background. His father, Harald, was a sculptor and Quistgaard learned to appreciate clean, classic lines from an early age. As a young man, he went to work for the silversmith Georg Jensen but it was his relationship with Nierenberg, whom he met in Copenhagen in 1954, that really changed his life. After seeing some of Quistgaard's stainless steel flatware, Nierenberg persuaded him to produce his designs for a mass-market audience through Dansk.

Although Quistgaard is credited with helping to bring enamelware back into fashion, it is for his teak designs that he has attracted the most attention. The beautiful Congo Ice Bucket (see opposite), designed in the 1950s, is based on the hull of a Viking ship and is highly collectable.

☞ **Items to look out for**

The original model sells at auction from about £200 (US $320) upwards. It is lined with red–orange plastic.

💧 **Top Tips**

You can still pick up models on eBay, but check the quality carefully.

A small version is 39cm (15.3in) in height.

🖳 **Websites**

Deconet
www.deconet.com

Maya
Tias Eckhoff

Created in the early 1960s, Maya is eminent Norwegian designer Tias Eckhoff's first cutlery pattern. The set was made at the request of Finn Henriksen, then owner and founder of kitchenware manufacturer Norstaal.

An award-winning design, Maya has been a best-selling cutlery series since 1962, when it was first released. Designed for comfort, with wide handles and tapering shapes, the cutlery is represented in design collections around the world, including the Victoria and Albert Museum (V&A) in London.

Born in southeastern Norway, Eckhoff studied to be a potter after leaving his Oslo-based school. He worked at the Porsgrund Porcelain works, where he was head designer from 1952. During that time, he designed the Det Riflede Series, which drew critical acclaim and established Eckhoff as a leading Norwegian designer.

In the 1950s, he began to design silverware, such as Cypress for the silversmith Georg Jensen. Its gentle curves and slightly concave handles made it popular with audiences. His Eckhoff Series, in stainless steel with palisandor, was designed for Danish company Dansk Knivfabrik in 1954. In this series, the bowl of the spoon was more egg shaped and the tines of the fork wider and shorter. Maya, the stainless steel cutlery designed for Norstaal, had a nearly circular spoon bowl and four very short but thin tines on the fork. It also had handles that were more fan shaped than in his previous designs. Its classic, clean look makes it popular with designers.

☞ Items to look out for

The original 1962 series, and not the more recent Maya 2000, which is longer and slimmer than its sister set. Both patterns are based on a triangular form, but Maya 2000 appears more streamlined.

● Top Tips

Stelton sells Eckhoff's Maya. A dinner spoon retails at about £17 (US $27) and a serving set at £73 (US $115).

▦ Websites

Stelton
www.stelton.com

Cylinda Tea Service
Arne Jacobsen

The master of classic, sleek and chic design, Arne Jacobsen turned his hand to everything from buildings and airports to lights, chairs, textiles and even ashtrays. He believed that even a coffee pot should be beautiful.

Arne Jacobsen studied architecture at the Royal Danish Academy of Fine Arts in Copenhagen and began his career by designing elegant single-family houses influenced by 19th-century Danish country architecture. Several high-profile commissions brought him to national and international prominence and he soon became known as an exponent of modernist architecture. In the late 1920s, Jacobsen worked with Flemming Lassen to create the cylindrical House of the Future for an exhibition in Copenhagen called Bygge-og Bolig Udstillingen i Forum. Over the following decades, his reputation as an influential designer grew through his designs for buildings and domestic ware.

The Cylinda Series was conceived from a sketch on a napkin in 1964. Taking three years to bring it into production, the series required new technology to make possible the stainless steel holloware and seamless, brushed surfaces that Jacobsen wanted. The perfection of the pieces in this collection – from the coffee pots and teapots to a pepper mill – are inspiring. The designer's attention to detail paid off when Cylinda won the Danish Society of Industrial Design ID award in 1967 and the American Institute of Interior Designers' International Design Award in 1968.

Items to look out for

An original Cylinda coffee pot may cost from £600 (US $960) upwards.

Top Tips

The Cylinda Series has been ripped off by various cheaper-selling designers. Look out for the seamless perfection of the original brushed-steel goods.

Websites

Stelton
www.stelton.com

Also See

■ Model 3107 (Series 7), pages 54–5;
  Egg Chair, pages 64–5;
  Swan Sofa, pages 66–7
■ Cutlery, pages 116–7
■ AJ Light, pages 144–5

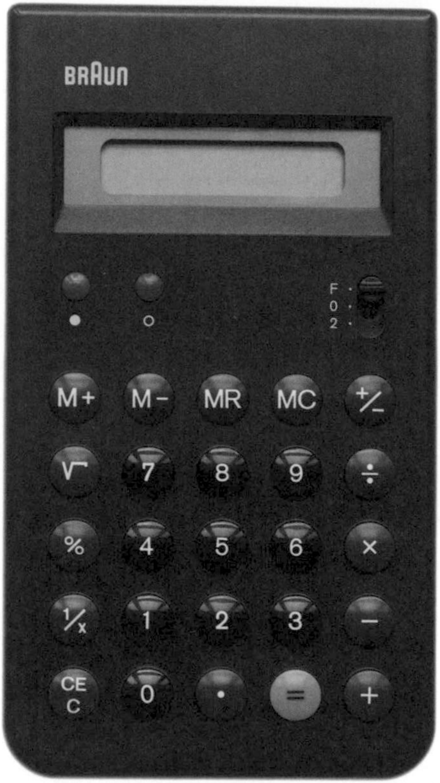
BRAUN
F
0
2
M+
M−
MR
MC
+/−
√
7
8
9
÷
%
4
5
6
×
1/x
1
2
3
−
CE C
0
•
=
+

ET44
Dieter Rams and Dietrich Lubs

It might seem odd to feature a calculator in a book on collectables, but the ET44 has been exhibited in various art collections around the world, including the Design Museum in London, which honoured it in its celebration of 25 years of design.

Created by Dieter Rams and Dietrich Lubs for German company Braun in the late 1970s, the ET44 calculator was one of several collaborations between the two men. The calculator is sleek, efficient and easy to use. In many ways, it sums up Dieter Rams's approach to good design. Arguably one of the most influential industrial designers of the late 20th century, Rams, as head for Braun, carefully defined what good design should be. He stated that it is 'innovative, aesthetic, unobtrusive, honest, long lasting, environmentally friendly, makes a product useful, makes a product understanding, is thorough down to the last detail and has as little design as possible'. Rams has also said that good designers must have an intuition about people's changing needs.

Braun and its design team fulfilled this need. In the post-war period, the company rose to prominence, creating innovative and cutting-edge designs that utilized the technological changes of the time. Rams and Lubs helped create the company's reputation for producing high-quality, well-designed small appliances in the 1970s and '80s, through items such as the ET44 calculator. So influential was the ET44's design that some people say that it has inspired the look of the calculator on Apple's iPhone.

Items to look out for

Although Braun developed other later calculators, the ET44 is the most iconic and desired by collectors.

Top Tips

Look for items still in their original boxes and with instructions.

Websites

Design Museum
designmuseum.org

Also See

■ 606 Universal Shelving System, pages 72–3

Teema
Kaj Franck

A talented designer, Kaj Franck is best known for his Kartio glassware and Teema (formerly Kilta) dinnerware. His designs are simple, classic and beautiful, aimed at best showcasing the items that are meant to placed in or on them.

Finnish designer Franck was a proponent of anonymity in design. This self-effacing view related particularly to utility products, which is reflected in his work.

In 1952, Finnish tableware company Arabia, where Franck worked as Head of Applied Arts, released his Kilta (Guild) Range. From its inception, Kilta challenged existing ideas about what a table service should be. The range was intended to fulfil the changing needs of the consumer who wanted tableware that was beautiful and easy to clean and store. The original service included jugs, cups, serving dishes and plates, and some pieces had interchangeable lids. The range was also stackable, to take up relatively little space, and geometrically shaped. The pieces were produced in single colours, which Franck, who referred to himself as an aesthetic tyrant, judged to be decoration enough. Kilta was produced until 1975.

In 1981, Kilta saw the light of day again, this time rebranded as Teema (Theme). Franck insisted on minor adjustments to the service to make it more suitable to the needs of the consumer. The dimensions of some of the pieces were altered and the range was produced in vitreous china to suit a modern household. More pieces were added in 2005.

☞ Items to look out for

Original Kilta products, particularly in white, blue, black, green or yellow.

The Cream Bottle with its cork stopper, which was designed to fit in a gap between people's windows before fridges became the norm. This bottle was discontinued in 2005.

The original Teema 18-piece set in white or black.

💡 Top Tips

From 2003 to 2005, Teema was sold by Iittala and Arabia before just being distributed by Iittala. Items from that period may become very collectable.

🖥 Websites

Iittala
www.iittala.com

Also See

■ **Nuutajärvi Notsjö**, pages 174–5

9091 Kettle
Richard Sapper

German-born designer Richard Sapper has become well known for his collaboration with Alessi. The 9091 Kettle, created for the Italian company, was the first designer product of this kind. It heralded a new age in kettle design.

Richard Sapper began designing for German car manufacturer Daimler-Benz in the 1950s. His creative impulse lies in designing products that people want to keep hold of for years – whether it be the Tizio 35 lamp or the IBM ThinkPad Laptop. His designs, Sapper says, have not just a point of view, but a personality as well.

Born in Germany, Sapper moved to Italy in the 1950s. He worked for architects Gio Ponti and Alberti Rosselli, before setting up his own studio in Milan. His influential work, on everything from a child's seat for Italian furniture producer Kartell to consulting on tyre design for Pirelli, helped build up Sapper's reputation as a man who never produced a bad design and led to him picking up many international design awards, including the Italian Compasso d'Oro 10 times.

The 9091 (Singing) Kettle, created for Alessi in 1983, is an expression of a belief that his products should be individual and unique. The stainless steel kettle is easy to both fill and pour from and can be used on a gas, ceramic or electric hob. Its distinctive melodic sound, generated from the brass whistle, is both E and B pitched. Sapper is said to have been inspired by the sound of steamships and barges sailing on the Rhine. It is often called the 'first designer kettle'.

☞ Items to look out for

A **9091 Kettle** retails at about £155 (US $248).

☀ Top Tips

The **distinctive brass whistle** gives this kettle an unusual sound.

▭ Websites

Alessi
www.alessi.com

Connox
www.connox.com

Also See

■ **Tizio 35**, pages 166–7

Global Knife
Komin Yamada

One of the most desired of kitchen implements, the Global Knife Series created a huge sensation when it was first released in the mid-1980s. The knives combined Japanese precision, German durability and Italian design aesthetics.

The forerunner to the Global Knife was the stainless steel Bunmei Gincho Knife produced by the Yoshida Metal Industry Co. Ltd in 1960. This popular knife's success lay in it being an easy-to-use product of a superior quality to those available on the market at the time. From this, came the idea of producing an entire knife – from the blade to the butt of the handle – out of a single piece of steel. The development of what would become the Global Knife Series began in the late 1970s and industrial designer Komin Yamada was commissioned to complete the brief of creating something stylish, precise and durable.

A combined treatment in which the metal is heated to 1,000°C (32°F) and then rapidly cooled was found to help increase the hardness of the blade. A second treatment then followed in which the metal endured another four hours of heat to make it even tougher. The knives that evolved had thinner and lighter blades than many European models and were also designed to be comfortable and effective to use – to this end Yamada designed a knife edge with a convex cross-sectional structure. The original series had 12 items and debuted on the European market in 1988. Since then, the Global Knife has won many international awards.

Items to look out for

The original knives produced in Japan in 1985.

The first series of 12 knives, which debuted in Europe at the Ambiente in Frankfurt, Germany.

Top Tips

Global Knives are made from one piece of metal, so avoid similar-shaped but inferior goods with seams.

They come with a lifetime guarantee. There are more inferior but similar products on the market, so check the manufacturer's guarantee.

Websites

Global Knives
www.global-knife.com

Grunwerg
www.grunwerg.co.uk

Warm
Brian Keaney and Tony Alfström

Created for Tonfisk Design, the porcelain and walnut Warm Series has been a huge success with design-conscious individuals. Contemporary and chic, the tableware from Keaney and Alfström's collection is very desirable.

The Irish–Finnish collaboration between Brian Keaney and Tony Alfström led to the establishment of the Finland-based Tonfisk Design company. Irish-born Keaney originally visited Norway on a four-month exchange programme, but rather than returning to Ireland, he moved to Finland instead and set up the internationally famous Tonfisk.

Believing that there was a gap for beautifully produced but functional tableware, Keaney and Alfström set about filling that space. Tonfisk's motto of 'Form follows function doesn't mean all objects have to look the same' has guided the designs that the company has developed. Aimed at design-conscious people between the ages of 25 and 60, Tonfisk's goods are practical but attractive.

Launched at the 2000 Ambiente fair in Frankfurt, the Warm tea and coffee service is made of high-quality porcelain encircled by bracelets of laminated walnut wood, which not only act as handles but also insulate the tea or coffee. On its release, Warm immediately grabbed public and media attention. Now made in walnut or oak and black or white ceramics, the service is a feature of design museums around the world. In 2010 further items were added to the series.

☞ Items to look out for

Since the Warm Series was introduced in the late 1990s, several cheaper ranges inspired by the design have come onto the market. The originals are made of laminated walnut wood and ultra-fine, high-quality porcelain.

☕ Top Tips

A further 14 items were added to the series in 2010, but these were not part of the original range.

Two 24cl (8.5floz) cups can cost £46 (US $75).

🖥 Websites

Skandium
www.skandium.com
Tonfisk
www.tonfisk-design.fi

BL1 Table Lamp (BestLite)
Robert Dudley Best

Designed by Robert Dudley Best, the BL1 Table Lamp, better known as the Bestlite, took its inspiration from Bauhaus. Winston Churchill famously had one on his desk in his Whitehall air-raid shelter during the Second World War.

Robert Dudley Best designed the BL1 Table Lamp, or Bestlite, in 1930. It quickly achieved fame and was reviewed in *The Architects' Journal* and hailed as the first manifestation of Bauhaus in England.

Dudley Best was heir to British company Best & Lloyd, one of the leading lighting factories in the world, but he drew his inspiration for the lamp from his exposure to French and German design. In 1925, he attended the International Exhibition of Modern Design in Paris, where he saw the designs of Le Corbusier and Ludwig Mies van der Rohe, and he studied at the Düsseldorf School of Industrial Design. It was during this time that he befriended Walter Gropius, head of Bauhaus, and first began to think of the design for the Bestlite.

Dudley Best returned to Birmingham, England, in 1930, where he persuaded his father to manufacture his work. The lamp, which was handmade, became known for its quality, clarity and elegance. The curved shade rotates and tilts through its axis and the arm similarly tilts up and down. Its functionality made it popular with customers such as the Royal Air Force. In 2004, Danish company Gubi took over Best & Lloyd; various models of the BL1 are still manufactured in Birmingham, England.

☞ **Items to look out for**

The original BL1 was a desk light and can be seen in the Design Museum in London.

● **Top Tips**

Today, other versions of the BL1 are available in black, white and ivory as a desk lamp, wall-mounted lamp and floor lamp, among other models.

A modern BL1 retails at about £319 (US $512).

🖳 **Websites**

Bestlite by Gubi
www.bestlite.dk

Gubi
www.gubi.com

Anglepoise 1227
George Carwardine

The Anglepoise's design draws on the constant tension principle of human limbs. It was designed to be energy saving yet stylish. One of the most popular 20th-century designs, the lamp is now also among the most copied.

English automotive engineer George Carwardine developed a new spring in 1932 that could remain in position after being moved in every direction. His more famous invention, the Anglepoise, was a lamp that could be repositioned to focus light In a chosen direction, supported and balanced by a series of these springs. The lamp was conceived almost as a by-product of this earlier idea. Carwardine licensed his design to Worcestershire-based manufacturer Herbert Terry & Sons, and the 1208, a single-tiered, four-spring industrial version, was introduced in 1934.

Terry produced the 1227, a three-spring version for the domestic market, in 1935. Much more stylish with a three-tiered Art Deco-inspired base made of Bakelite and a shade and arm of lacquered steel, it could take a 25-watt rather than 60-watt bulb and was energy saving. In 1938, a new 1227 appeared with a two-tiered base and a wider shade that was capable of taking a 40-watt bulb.

Terry commissioned British designer Kenneth Grange to revamp the original 1227 and his 2003 Anglepoise Type 3 has a double-skin shade that can take a 100-watt bulb. A limited edition Giant 1227 Floor Lamp, nearly 2.75m (9ft) high, became available in 2004.

☞ **Items to look out for**

The original Anglepoise 1227 had a three-tiered Bakelite base and shade; the 1938 1227 has two tiers. Authentic shades were black, white or occasionally red, canary yellow or green in a stone enamel finish.

● **Top Tips**

The Anglepoise is one of the most copied lamps. Most modern Anglepoises are all metal and available in a range of colours with a solid circular base or a screw clamp.

The Type 3 is an updated version of the classic Anglepoise 1227.

An early 1227 retails at a minimum of about £300 (US $500). The later two-tiered version can be found for about £150 (US $240).

🔲 **Websites**

Anglepoise
www.anglepoise.com
SCP
www.scp.co.uk

AJ Light
Arne Jacobsen

So many of Arne Jacobsen's iconic designs saw the light of day because of his commission to create the SAS Royal Hotel in Copenhagen – and the AJ Light is no exception.

Jacobsen worked on the exterior and interior designs for the SAS Royal Hotel between 1958 and 1960. What he produced was little short of a design miracle. Jacobsen's attention to detail – from the ashtrays in which guests would stub out their cigarettes to the cutlery with which they would eat and also the lighting of the hotel – would influence and shape modern design over the following decades.

The AJ Table and Floor Lights were introduced in 1960. They provide direct and angled illumination, the latter through the tiltable and asymmetrical head design. The lamp consists of a conic metal shade, an enamelled brass pipe with a tilting mechanism and a heavy base. When the lamp is pointed downwards, the edge of the shade is horizontal and the light source is effectively screened from the user. The inside of the shade is matt white enamel.

The light's shape was designed to complement and echo the design of Jacobsen's Egg and Swan Chairs. The cut-out in the heavy base of the light was designed to fit an ashtray, although this design feature is attractive and distinctive enough without that item in place.

Louis Poulsen introduced a new range to celebrate the 50th anniversary of the AJ Light in 2010.

☞ **Items to look out for**

The original AJ Lights are very hard to find. Be prepared to pay upwards of £2,000 (US $3,200).

The new range of colours of the 50th Anniversary Range.

📍 **Top Tips**

More modern versions in inferior materials are available. Check the provenance properly before buying.

The 50th Anniversary Lights produced by Louis Poulsen in petroleum, red, sand, yellow–green and blue–green: the AJ Table Lamp is £625 (US $1,000) and the AJ Floor Lamp is £710 (US $1,135).

🌐 **Websites**

Skandium
www.skandium.com
Louis Poulsen
www.louis-poulsen.co.uk

Also See

■ Model 3107 (Series 7), pages 54–5; Swan Sofa, pages 66–7

■ Cutlery, pages 116–7;

PH5
Pøul Henningsen

Scandinavian designers have given us many modern classics, yet few pieces have achieved the iconic status of Pøul Henningsen's PH Series. Recognized throughout the world, the PH light fittings are great examples of industrial design.

Born in Denmark in 1894, Pøul Henningsen initially trained as an architect but soon became fascinated by the exciting new technology of the electric light bulb and decided to dedicate himself to producing innovative light fittings. He aimed to recreate the soft gas-lighting effect that he had known as a child, as his hometown had no electricity when he was a boy.

He collaborated with Louis Poulsen & Co, a firm that sold tools and electrical supplies to develop a lamp for the modern lighting competition of the International Exhibition of Modern Design in Paris (1925). The PH Lamp won first prize. Based on studies of light and shade distribution, it was designed to avoid glare.

Released in 1926, the PH design was a success and Henningsen subsequently expanded his range. The PH5 (1958) was made to hang low over a table and give moderate illumination. The '5' refers to 5dm (50cm/19.7in), the diameter of the top shade. Made of three reflective shades, the smaller two coloured shades were red and blue because they belong to the colour spectrum to which the human eye is least sensitive. Light is diffused through a sandblasted glass shield in the lower shade and the visible reflectors direct light both vertically and horizontally. It is also glare free.

☞ **Items to look out for**

The original PH lampshade. Expect to pay £250 (US $400) for a new one, but it is possible to buy second-hand originals.

Top Tips

The best place to look for a second-hand PH lampshade is eBay; however, beware of reproductions often made in China.

Rewiring the lamp does not affect its value and makes it safer to use. Try to use authentic cloth-covered wire, though.

Websites

Louis Poulsen
www.louis-poulsen.co.uk

Also See

■ PH Artichoke, pages 148–9

PH Artichoke
Pøul Henningsen

Developed for the Langelinie Pavillonen in Copenhagen, where it can still be found, the PH Artichoke is a masterpiece of 20th-century lighting design. It has been much copied but the original Henningsen light is still incomparable.

Pøul Henningsen was the son of famous Danish actress Agnes Henningsen. He studied but never graduated as an architect and pursued a number of professions before he began his long collaboration with the influential Louis Poulsen, for whom he produced the celebrated PH Series. Henningsen designed the PH Artichoke to sit grandly in a beautiful Copenhagen eatery, Langelinie Pavillonen, where it can still be found hanging in majestic splendour alongside Arne Jacobsen's chairs and Børge Mogensen's sofas.

Developed in the 1950s, its design is made from 12 steel arches on which 72 copper leaves are placed in 12 circular rows with 6 blades in each row, so the light source is effectively hidden from the viewer. Each row is staggered so that each of the 72 leaves covers each other. Henningsen's light is 360-degrees glare free and the leaves cleverly reflect and redirect light onto each other and the next level of copper leaves. This is helped by an inner chrome diffuser and creates an innovative and impressive light fixture for anyone viewing it.

Today, the PH Artichoke, named after the vegetable that it resembles, is a design classic. Much desired by collectors, Henningsen's elegant and majestic light showcases Scandinavian lighting design at its best.

☞ Items to look out for

Henningsen's majestic PH Artichoke is composed of leaflike elements and, with its grand size, is ideal for larger settings. It is almost as expensive as it is beautiful, however. Expect to pay £7,000 (US $11,200) for an original if you are lucky.

♥ Top Tips

The original lights didn't have cables (see opposite).

There are a number of cheaper products available claiming to be the PH Artichoke. This light is expensive and it is an investment.

▭ Websites

Louis Poulsen
www.louis-poulsen.co.uk

Also See
■ **PH5**, pages 146–7

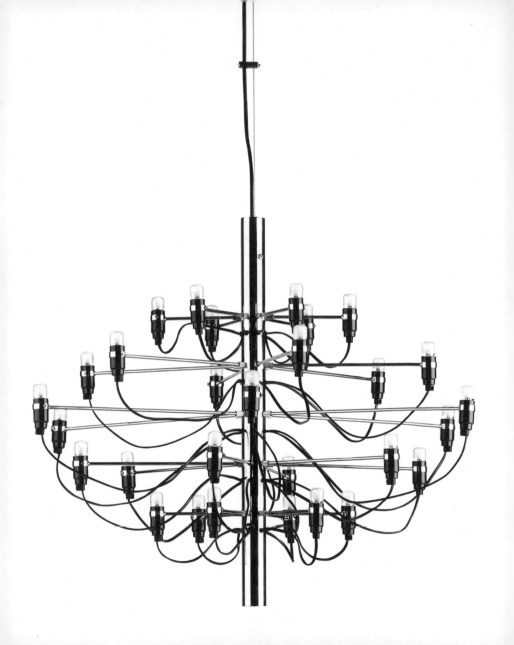

2097 Chandelier
Gino Sarfatti

For most of his impressive career, Gino Sarfatti was obsessed with the light bulb. In pretty much all of his designs the light source is the most important element, as exemplified by his 2097 Chandelier.

Although Italian light designer Gino Sarfatti began taking aeronaval studies at university, he did not complete his degree and instead ended up working in a glass shop in Milan. It was there that his fascination with glass and lighting probably began. In 1938, he created his first light source and in the following year he founded his own workshop, Arteluce. Although his work was disrupted by the outbreak of the Second World War and his departure from Italy to Switzerland, Sarfatti returned to Milan in 1945 and resumed his experiments with light.

In the post-war period, Arteluce was at the forefront of lighting design, attracting young and talented men and women to work for the company. From the early 1950s, Sarfatti began to utilize plexiglass and later adopted the use of halogens in his light fittings.

In 1958, Sarfatti developed possibly one of his most recognized light fixtures, the 2097 Chandelier. Made of a central steel structure equipped with brass arms and suspension cables, this striking chandelier is a fitting that diffuses light.

Sarfatti sold Arteluce to Italian light company Flos. The 2097 Chandelier has spawned various cheaper models but Sarfatti's light remains a collector's dream.

☞ Items to look out for

The 2097 is available in chrome and brass. It retails from about £1,092 (US $1,750) for a small version (30 bulbs); a large version (50 bulbs) can cost £1,719 (US $2,750).

● Top Tips

The original 2097 is made of steel and brass. Much lighter, far cheaper models are also available.

Websites

Flos
www.flos.com
The Conran Shop
www.conranshop.co.uk

Moon Lamp
Verner Panton

A master of form, shape and colour, Verner Panton was one of Denmark's most influential designers. His distinctive modular designs, vivid colour palette and space-age creations perfectly summed up the landscape of the 1950s and '60s.

Like many famous Scandinavian designers, Verner Panton trained as an architect, and the clean lines and curves of his light fittings and furniture often pay a nod to that early training.

Although Panton was friends with some of the leading Danish designers of the mid-20th century, including Arne Jacobsen, whom he assisted for two years in the early 1950s, and fellow lighting specialist Pøul Henningsen, he wanted to make his own individual mark on the international design scene. Using modern materials such as plastics and the vivid colours and challenging shapes associated with Pop Art, Panton quickly became famous as an innovative and cutting-edge designer. The Moon Lamp, which he produced in 1960, is one of the creations that helped him achieve recognition and success.

It is made up of 10 ring-shaped, white lacquered metal discs that are suspended around the central light source in such a way that the elements can move. Today, there are versions made in plastic too. The fan-shaped discs cover the light source from view but also act as reflectors. Light also filters through the gaps in the discs so that a soft 'moonlike' light diffuses through the space the lamp inhabits.

☞ **Items to look out for**
The original 1960 Moon Lamp.

🏆 **Top Tips**
While it is still possible to find an original Moon Lamp on auction sites, check its provenance carefully. Very good modern reproductions exist, most often made of plastic.

🌐 **Websites**
Frandsen Group
www.frandsengroup.dk
Verner Panton Museum
www.vernerpanton.com
Vitra
www.vitra.com

Also See
- **Panton Stacking Chair**, pages 80–1
- **FlowerPot**, pages 160–1;
  VP Globe, pages 162–3;
  Spiral Triple SP3, pages 164–5

Arco Floor Light
Achille and Pier Giacomo Castiglioni

One of the most recognizable – and also copied – of Achille and Pier Giacomo's designs for Flos, the Arco Floor Light combines style and elegance with functionality – reasons why it remains popular with design audiences.

Born in Milan, Italy, Achille Castiglioni and his brothers Livio and Pier Giacomo began to experiment with industrial design as early as the 1940s. Working with the Italian lighting company Flos, Achille and Pier Giacomo devised some of the best of Italian mid-20th-century designs, including the 1962 Arco Floor Light.

The Castiglioni brothers originally designed the lamp because of Achille's frustration with the table lamp. At that time, most lighting fixtures dangled from a central fitting, usually in the middle of a room. However, if one wanted to light a table, for example, for a dinner party, an ugly lead would trail across the floor. Achille thus struggled to find a solution to what he deemed was a very unattractive problem. The Arco Floor Light was the result.

Made from high-quality materials, the Arco was all about style and functionality. Essentially a lamp that provided direct light, the Arco Floor Light had a white Carrara marble block for the base. The marble, from an area in the Italian Alps, was reportedly Renaissance artist Michelangelo's favourite material. The height-adjustable Arco Floor Light has a satin-finish stainless steel telescopic stem and the light source lies within a zapon-varnished, swivelling aluminium reflector.

☞ **Items to look out for**

Original Arco Lights can cost upwards of £1,600 (US $2,566).

💡 **Top Tips**

There are many Arco-inspired lights on the market and if you can't afford the real thing it is possible to find a good reproduction for about £100 to £150 (US $160–240).

The base of a real Arco Floor Light is made of Carrara marble.

🌐 **Websites**

Flos
www.flos.com

Y Lighting
www.ylighting.com

Also See

■ Snoopy Table Lamp, pages 158–9;
Taraxacum 88 Chandelier,
pages 168–9

Spider 291
Joe Colombo

Everything Italian master Joe Colombo designed in his short but productive 41 years was intended to be created for an environment 'of the future'. Colombo's talent and enthusiasm resulted in great innovative design such as the Spider 291.

Cesare Colombo, better known as 'Joe', was born in Milan in 1930. His father was an industrialist. As a young man, Colombo had an interest in both science and art; this combination would inform his work as a professional industrial designer.

In 1953, he produced a ceiling for a jazz club in Milan, thus embarking on his first industrial design project. When his father became ill, Colombo and his younger brother Gianni took on the running of his electrical conductor manufacturing company. Colombo turned this opportunity to his own advantage, using the time to experiment with new materials such as fibreglass and polyvinyl chloride (PVC). In 1962, he set up his own design studio and concentrated on making products for the fluid lifestyle of the new emerging society. He merged new production processes with new materials to create seating, containers and lighting.

In 1965, Colombo designed the Spider 291, for which he won the Compasso d'Oro and AID International Design Award two years later. The design has an enamelled metal base, a chrome-plated tubular metal stem and an enamelled shade with a melamine fitting. It also featured an innovative plastic joint, allowing the horizontal spotlight to be rotated and tilted.

☞ **Items to look out for**

The original 291 made for Oluce.

♥ **Top Tips**

Pretty much all of Joe Colombo's designs are collectable if you can find them.

A modern Oluce-produced Spider 291 can cost about £490 (US $785). It is available in black or white.

▭ **Websites**

Oluce
www.oluce.com

Snoopy Table Lamp
Achille and Pier Giacomo Castiglioni

Probably more famous for designing the iconic Arco Floor Light, brothers Achille and Pier Giacomo Castiglioni also created the conceptual Snoopy Table Lamp in 1967.

The three Castiglioni brothers, Livio, Pier Giacomo and Achille, all trained as architects. Livio and Pier Giacomo established a studio in the early 1940s, which Achille, the youngest brother, joined in 1944. Eight years later, oldest brother Livio broke away to set up his own studio. The collaboration between Achille and Pier Giacomo continued successfully for many years. Pier Giacomo was considered to be the more intellectual of the two and later taught architectural composition and design at the Polytechnic of Milan until his death in 1968.

Together, Achille and Pier Giacomo won many accolades. They have the distinction of having six of their works in a permanent exhibition at the Museum of Modern Art (MoMA) in New York and the brothers also won several awards.

Designed in the 1960s, the Snoopy Table Lamp uses the best materials possible but combines functionality with fun. Similar to the Castiglionis' stylish Arco Floor Light from 1962, the Snoopy has a base made from the beautiful and high-quality white-and-grey Carrara marble. The lamp was designed to provide direct light and features an integral touch dimmer in the base and an enamelled black metal reflector.

☞ **Items to look out for**

The Snoopy Table Lamp can cost upwards of £600 (US $960).

💡 **Top Tips**

A new version of the Snoopy was brought out for Euroluce 2003. It is not to be confused with the original c.1967 Flos version.

Websites

Flos
www.flos.com
Y Lighting
www.ylighting.com

Also See

■ Arco Floor Light, pages 154–5;
Taraxacum 88 Chandelier,
pages 168–9

FlowerPot
Verner Panton

Instantly recognizable, FlowerPot lights have inspired generations of industrial designers since they were first created. Produced in vividly coloured plastic, the lights instantly scream Danish designer Verner Panton's name.

Arguably, Arne Jacobsen had the most influence over Verner Panton's evolution into a world-renowned designer. Jacobsen was Panton's mentor and boss at his architect's practice during the early 1950s. Although Panton's work after that period is as different as one could possibly get from Jacobsen's, he learned a great amount about form, structure and substance during those years.

Panton's shapes, colours and materials define the kind of designer he became – his creations have come to symbolize the '60s, as seen in the FlowerPot, produced in 1968. His second mass-produced light (after the Topan), the FlowerPot seemingly fulfilled his desire to 'provoke people into using their imagination and make their surroundings more exciting'.

The FlowerPot consists of two hemispheres that face each other. The diameter of the upper hemisphere is twice that of the lower one. The lower hemisphere also hides the light source and both of their exteriors serve as colourful reflecting surfaces.

Initially made of enamelled industrial metal, the FlowerPot was available in turquoise, white, red and orange or polished steel. Verner Panton's light won the West German Bundespries Gute Award in 1972.

☞ Items to look out for

Made in a range of vivid colours, today a large FlowerPot pendant light (h. 30cm/12in; d. 50cm/19.7in) can fetch more than £1,250 (US $2,000). A modern version can be found for about £177 (US $285).

● Top Tips

The light is available in yellow, orange, red, black, turquoise, blue, white, brown, chrome, and brushed steel.

The original light was made by Louis Poulsen.

🔲 Websites

Heal's
www.heals.co.uk
Skandium
www.skandium.com

Also See

◼ **Panton Stacking Chair**, pages 80–1

◼ **AJ Light**, pages 144–5;
Moon Lamp, pages 152–3;
VP Globe, pages 162–3

VP Globe
Verner Panton

Multi-talented Verner Panton had a career spanning more than five decades. His designs – whether they be the Panton Stacking Chair or the VP Globe – can be seen in museums around the world.

Danish designer Verner Panton had already achieved cult status for creations such as the Topan and the colourful FlowerPot lights and had picked up many international awards when he designed the VP Globe. An object that is almost sculptural, the Globe has to be viewed in situ in a high-ceiling modern landscape to be fully appreciated.

A master innovator always looking for a new shape, a new material and a fresh opportunity to push the boundaries further, Panton designed the VP Globe in the late 1960s. The transparent acrylic sphere of the light fitting surrounds five internal white or coloured plates, which reflect and radiate light, diffusing it around the room.

The concave/convex aluminium dishes of various sizes, lacquered white and suspended on micro steel-ball chains, are encapsulated like a bottled ship inside the acrylic sphere. Arguably deconstructing Pøul Henningsen's PH Lights, of which it is reminiscent, the VP Globe is elegant but also innovative. Panton designed the light originally for Louis Poulsen, who had first manufactured the PH lights. The VP Globe remains as popular today with audiences as it was when first released.

☞ Items to look out for

The licensed product stamped with the designer's signature and with a certificate of authenticity.

☻ Top Tips

The light was reissued – the Panton Globe (all white interior) and the VP Globe (with a splash of red and blue) are available for about £1,370 (US $2,195) for the 40cm (15.5in) diameter and about £1,720 (US $2,750) for the 50cm (19.5in) diameter.

🔲 Websites

Design Within Reach
www.dwr.com

Frandsen Group
www.frandsengroup.dk

VerPan
www.verpan.dk

Also See

■ **Panton Stacking Chair**, pages 80–1

■ **Moon Lamp**, pages 152–3;
FlowerPot, pages 160–1;
Spiral Triple SP3, pages 164–5

Spiral Triple SP3
Verner Panton

Named the enfant terrible of Danish design, Verner Panton pushed the boundaries of what was previously acceptable, using new materials, colours and shapes to make everyday objects interesting for a mass-market audience.

Although a native Dane, Verner Panton spent most of his life after the early 1960s living and working in Basel, Switzerland. It was there that many of his futuristic, idea-challenging chairs, lighting and other interior designs were produced. Panton challenged perception – as seen famously in his Phantasy Landscape, which was made up of a room of foam-rubber organic shapes, designed for the 1970 Visiona II Exhibition in Cologne.

Panton believed that 'a less successful experiment is preferable to a beautiful platitude.' And through his designs, he sought to provide an alternative to the stylistically unchallenged, uniform interior with the use of colour, shape, unorthodox materials and designs that altered spatial perception and that could often be manipulated and moved. Thus, a light fitting could alter the ambience of a room just by being bent or made to sway. Panton's designs also often brought a sense of fun to an otherwise bland or staid interior. This can be seen in his Spiral Lamps from the late '60s, which are made up of plastic spirals of different lengths arranged to form spheroid shapes. The Spiral Triple SP3, in particular, made of metal and the plastic cellidor, is highly sculptural. The spirals in its three spheroids are attached to each other by nylon threads.

☞ **Items to look out for**

The white or silver cellidor SP3 can retail at upwards of £2,800 (US $4,500).

● **Top Tips**

More modern versions appear in other colours such as gold and are made by VerPan, a Danish company specializing in Panton's designs.

www **Websites**

Frandsen Group
www.frandsengroup.com
VerPan
www.verpan.dk

Also See

■ **Panton Stacking Chair,** pages 80–1
■ **Moon Lamp,** pages 152–3;
FlowerPot, pages 160–1;
VP Globe, pages 162–3

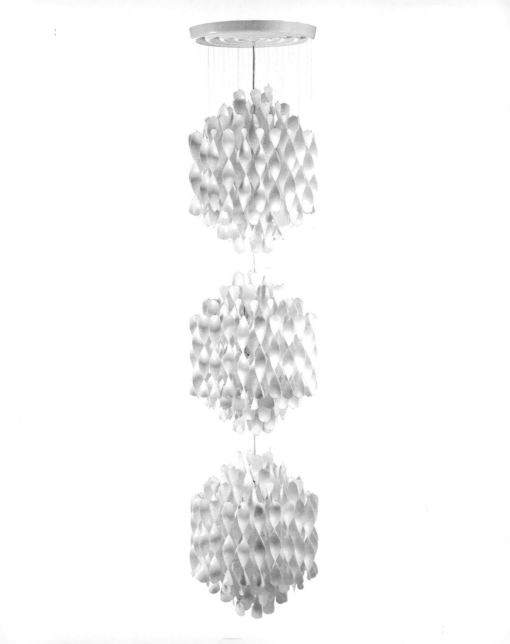

Tizio 35
Richard Sapper

Richard Sapper's Tizio 35 is considered by many to be one of the finest lighting designs of the second half of the 20th century. Sapper is also known for the beautiful Singing 9091 Kettle produced for Alessi, among other designs.

German-born Richard Sapper lives and works in Milan. Although he had a successful collaboration with Italian industrial designer Marco Zanuso, Sapper set up his own design studio, where he created several iconic designs. The Tizio 35 is a lamp from that period and was created in 1972.

Sapper designed the Tizio 35 for Italian design company Artemide. Featured in many of the best design collections around the world, the Tizio 35 was Sapper's attempt at redesigning the common desk lamp. In doing so, he created an innovative design that was adjustable and able to throw out intense but precise light from what was a very small light source. The lamp also used a halogen light source, one of the first to be used outside the car industry.

Sapper incorporated a very sensitive counterweight system that allowed the movable and adjustable arm of the lamp to be put into practically any position desired. This feature enabled the user to have total control over the direction of the light generated by the lamp. Electricity was conducted via the arms to the light source, thus eliminating the need for an unsightly cable. Sapper's light also incorporated a low-voltage transformer in its base.

☞ **Items to look out for**

The original Tizio 35.

♟ **Top Tips**

The Tizio 35 is available in grey for about £241 (US $385), black for about £256 (US $410) and white metallic for about £225 (US $360).

www **Websites**

Artemide
www.artemide.com
Ylighting
www.ylighting.com

Also See

■ **9091 Kettle**, pages 134–5

Taraxacum 88 Chandelier
Achille Castiglioni

The stunning Taraxacum 88 Chandelier is but one of the many successful designs that Italian master Achille Castiglioni created. He named it after the Latin word for 'dandelion', which the light fitting closely resembles.

The three Castiglioni brothers, Achille, Livio and Pier Giacomo, became known for their innovative, elegant but smart designs. They worked from the maxim: 'Start from scratch. Stick to common sense. Know your goals and means.' Thus, they were able to create iconic products for Flos such as the Arco Floor Light and the Taraxacum 88 Chandelier, often mixing and merging existing accepted forms with each other to create newer, better and sleeker products that were more efficient yet still visually challenging.

The brothers believed that the best of the old could be mixed with the new without compromising quality. They also thought it was important to have a constant and consistent way of design and not a particular style. This principle helped their creative process to evolve continually, which shines through in their light fittings.

The Taraxacum 88 Chandelier was designed by Achille Castiglioni in the 1980s and manufactured by Flos. It provides direct and reflected light. Made of 20 pressed and polished aluminium triangles, the S1 fitting has 60 clear Globolux light bulbs fixed around the structure; the S2 features 120 bulbs. The ceiling fitting, suspension cable and rose of this extraordinary lamp are made of steel.

☞ Items to look out for

The original light can retail at upwards of £4,000 (US $6,230) if you are lucky.

♟ Top Tips

The Taraxacum 88 is a modern collectable and an investment. It needs a large space to maximize its beauty and lighting potential.

The S1 retails at about £1,980 (US $3,170); the S2 at about £3,920 (US $6,270).

www Websites

Flos
www.flos.com
The Conran Shop
www.conran.com

Also See

■ Arco Floor Light, pages 154–5; Snoopy Table Lamp, pages 158–9

ARA
Philippe Starck

Possibly best known for his influential and instantly recognizable designs for the Italian company Alessi, Philippe Starck has produced a host of other products, including the ARA, that feature in design museums around the world.

Philippe Starck is almost a byword for modern design, and he is famous for rethinking and reworking old objects in new ways. Pretty much everyone at some point has owned a product designed or inspired by Starck, whether it be a Juicy Salif Lemon Squeezer, an Alessi Corkscrew or if he or she is lucky an ARA.

Born in 1949, in Paris, Starck was inspired to design by his aircraft designer father, who let his son play around with materials. In the 1960s, Starck's inflatable furniture began to attract attention. His reputation grew when he fitted out the celebrated Parisian nightclub Les Bains-Douches and when French president François Mitterrand commissioned him to decorate a suite in the presidential palace.

In 1988, Starck designed the ARA (his daughter shares the same name) and immediately received acclaim for this work. The elegant and balanced design, the polished finish and the conical horn shape all make the ARA eminently desirable by design-conscious consumers. It is so sleekly and seamlessly crafted that users may find it hard to find the on–off switch. The switch is in fact integrated into the lamp head – one just has to tilt the horn upwards to switch it off and tilt it back down to switch it on.

☞ **Items to look out for**

A modern design classic, the ARA is guaranteed to rise in value as well as add class and elegance to any office or residence.

🍃 **Top Tips**

The ARA can sell for between £370 and £550 (US $595–875).

🖵 **Websites**

Flos
www.flos.com
Starck's own website
www.philippestarck.com

Savoy Vase
Alvar Aalto

Probably one of the most recognized of Alvar Aalto's designs, the Savoy Vase is named after Helsinki's Savoy Restaurant, for which Aalto and his wife, Aino Marsio, designed fixtures and fittings in 1937.

Although an established architect, already gaining a reputation for design after producing the 41 Paimio chair for a tuberculosis (TB) sanatorium, Aalto felt his work was largely overlooked in his homeland, Finland. In 1935, the Aaltos moved to Helsinki, where they set up the design company Artek to capitalize on the designs they had produced for the sanatorium. In 1937, Aalto won an architectural commission to design the Savoy Restaurant in the city. The glassware collection that he subsequently produced, and which was presented at the Paris Exposition in that same year, won great acclaim.

The Savoy Vase evokes the landscape of Finland – although the designer said that it was inspired by the breeches of a young Inuit girl. The earliest models were made from recycled glass, which lent a greenish tinge to their appearance. They were mouth blown around a wooden template, which produced an uneven finish. The folds in the glass resulted in any flowers placed in the vase falling away from each other – thus facing towards the diners seated at the tables in the restaurant. The Finnish company Iittala continues to produce the vase but uses metal templates, although each piece is still individually blown.

☞ **Items to look out for**

The original vase was 14cm (5.5in) high and made from recycled glass; subsequently Iittala have released versions in different heights and colours.

💡 **Top Tips**

More modern versions are made using a metal template. They retail at between £43 (US $70) for a 9.5cm (3.75in) version and £99 (US $160) for a 16cm (6.3in) version.

www **Websites**

Iittala
www.iittala.com

Skandium
www.skandium.com

Also See

▣ **41 Paimio**, pages 20–1

▣ **Tea Trolley 901**, pages 96–7

Nuutajärvi Notsjö
Kaj Franck

Kaj Franck is often described as the conscience of Finnish design. An internationally renowned and award-winning designer, Franck produced some of his finest work for the Nuutajärvi Notsjö glassworks.

Nuutajärvi is the oldest glassworks in Finland, established in 1793 in Urjala by Jacob Wilhelm de Pont and Harald Furnhjelm. Originally, it specialized in bottles and glass for windows. The company changed hands several times before it was bought by the Wärtsilä Group in 1950. Some extremely fine designers have worked there, including Kaj Franck, who was its chief designer from the 1950s to 1976. The company merged with Iittala in 1988 and its glass is now sold under that name.

Although the company had been going for more than 150 years by the time Franck came to work there, it was under his guidance that some of the most beautiful glassware was produced. Franck, who was born in Vyborg, believed in paring down design to the key essentials. His designs are simple, fluid and geometrically balanced and often focus on items made for everyday use.

Today Franck is probably most famous for his Kartio glass series and the Teema Range of tableware, but glassware such as the dark purple KF 260 Vase (see opposite), produced in 1959, showcases his elegant, streamlined artistry at its best. It is also becoming increasingly collectable.

☞ **Items to look out for**

The KF 260 (1959) has a diameter of 11.5cm (4.5in). It can be found on auction sites for as little as £240 (US $390).

💡 **Top Tips**

Look out for the engraving 'K Franck Nuutajärvi Notsjö' and the year on the base of the vase.

🌐 **Websites**

Iittala
www.iittala.com

Modernist Glass
www.modernistglass.com

Also See

■ **Teema**, pages 132–3

Holmegaard
Per Lütken

In recent years, Scandinavian glass has become extremely popular with design audiences. Among them Holmegaard, with its crisp lines and lovely jewel-toned glass, has risen to the fore. Per Lütken was its chief designer from 1942 to 1998.

When it first opened its doors in Zealand in 1825, the Danish Holmegaard Glass Company, which was founded by Countess Henriette Danneskiold-Samsøe, made bottles. Over the years, the company's repertoire has expanded to include decorative glass and it subsequently attracted some of the world's finest designers, including Jacob E. Bang.

For many people, Holmegaard really came into its own under the direction of Per Lütken, who joined the company in 1942, stepping into Bang's talented shoes. He worked at the glassworks for more than five decades until his death in 1998.

Lütken's understanding of and feeling for glass were superlative and Holmegaard reached new heights in terms of product design under his direction. Utilizing classic methods, such as blowing hot glass with a pin, he created innovative and beautiful glassware, resulting in a whole line of art glass in the late 1950s.

Among Lütken's most sought-after work is the 1959 Duckling Vase, which is budlike and asymmetrical, and the classic Carnaby Range (1968), which was released in vivid colours such as red, yellow and white, lined with opaque white, in geometrically influenced shapes. They have an almost plastic finish to them.

☞ **Items to look out for**

Holmegaard glass such as the Duckling Vase (1950s), Flamingo Vases (1956), coloured and cased, and the popular Pop Art-influenced Carnaby Range (1968) are particularly collectable, ranging from upwards of £300 ($500), depending on their size and condition.

Top Tips

Auction sites such as eBay are still very good places to find Holmegaard glass.

Beware of sellers touting 'Holmegaard-era' glass as this doesn't necessarily mean they are selling the real thing.

The Carnaby Range is not to be confused with Michael Bang's 1970 Palet Range or Otto Brauer's 1962 Gulvvase Bottle Vases for Kastrup, which were produced by Kastrup and Holmegaard after they merged in 1965 and inspired by Per Lütken's work.

Websites

20th Century Glass
www.20thcenturyglass.com

Orrefors

Scandinavian designers of the 1950s and 1960s produced glass that had an unusual clarity and fluidity, establishing their reputation around the world. Among the market leaders were the talented people working at Orrefors.

After the Second World War, the Swedish company Orrefors employed several very talented designers, producing very sought-after work. Although some of the work was mass produced and can be found for less than £200 ($300), Orrefors designs remain highly collectable. Ingeborg Lundin, who joined Orrefors in 1947, produced, among other designs, the celebrated free-blown Apple Vase in 1955 (see opposite). It has been called the 'world's best-known piece of 1950s' glass'. She became known as the 'Balenciaga of glass', a reference to the renowned Spanish fashion designer Cristóbal Balenciaga.

Another woman who has helped keep Orrefors's designs on the map is Stockholm-born Ingegerd Råman. An award-winning designer, her work is held by eminent institutions such as the National Museum in Stockholm, the Victoria and Albert Museum (V&A) in London and the Corning Museum of Glass in New York. Råman joined Orrefors in 1999 and has received many awards for her work. Her designs are recognizable for their clarity and fluidity. She has commented that there is always a 'link between simplicity, function and aesthetic values' in her work and that they do not come truly to life until they are used. Thus, her work often has several uses – the lid of a jug is also a drinking glass and a carafe may be used as a vase.

☞ Items to look out for

Ingeborg Lundin's Apple Vase (1955). It is 37cm (15in) high and can cost from £2,500 to £5,000 (US $4,000–8,000). The green version is the most expensive.

Other Orrefors goods of note are the designs of Nils Landberg (Tulip Glass Range from 1957).

♥ Top Tips

Ingegerd Råman's work is available from shops such as Skandium.

▦ Websites

Jacksons
www.jacksons.se
Orrefors
www.orrefors.com
Skandium
www.skandium.com

Riihimäki/Riihimäen Lasi Oy

After the Second World War, the Finnish glass company Riihimäki employed many female designers, including Nanny Still, Helena Tynell and Tamara Aladin. The work of these women is in great demand today.

The idea for a glassworks near the town of Riihimäki came from a wish to promote Finnish industries. By the late 1930s, Riihimäki glassworks was the second largest in Scandinavia and Riihimäki became known as the Crystal City. The glassworks' designs came to particular prominence after taking the Grand Prix at Barcelona in 1928, tipping Orrefors (see previous entry) off its place as the leading Scandinavian glassworks.

Under Arttu Brummer's direction, most of the leading names in glassware were trained and the company became famous for producing striking, bold and innovative glassware. In particular, the work of its main designers Nanny Still, Helena Tynell and Aimo Okkolin and later designers Tamara Aladin and Erkkitapio Siiroinen are desirable to collectors today.

Geometrical and available in a range of stunning colours, most of these designers' pieces were mould blown, which allowed them to be mass produced and therefore available to a more general audience internationally.

Although it is still possible to buy work by these designers for very little investment, some pieces, such as the Moon landing-inspired Apollo Lamp by Tamara Aladin, Erkkitapio Siiroinen's 1970 Kasperi Vases and Nanny Still's beautiful Grapponia pieces of art glass are more expensive.

☞ **Items to look out for**

Any art glass from Nanny Still, Helena Tynell, Tamara Aladin, Aimo Okkolin and Arttu Brummer.

Original Tamara Aladin vases (for example the Green Glass Hoop Vase opposite) can be found for as little as £30 (US $48) if you shop carefully. Aladin's 1969 two-piece Apollo Vase, in clear and red glass, can be found for about £75 (US $120); Erkkitapio Siiroinen's 1970 Kasperi Vase can be found for about £85 (US $135).

♀ **Top Tips**

Watch out for modern reproductions. A number of sellers on popular internet trader sites claim vases are Riihimäki when they are in fact modern mass-market cheaper rip-offs.

🖦 **Websites**

eBay
www.ebay.co.uk
20th Century Glass
www.20thcenturyglass.com

Whitefriars Glass
Geoffrey Baxter

British glassworks Whitefriars has a long tradition of producing high-quality glass. Recognized for its vibrant and innovative designs, particularly those by Geoffrey Baxter, Whitefriars Glass is very desirable.

The small glassworks that became Whitefriars in 1963 began operating in 1720 in a small space in London's Fleet Street. In 1834, the glassworks was purchased by James Powell, a London wine merchant, and traded as James Powell & Sons. By the late 1850s, the firm had begun to design and produce the domestic table glass for which it is best known today. In 1923, the company moved to Wealdstone, near Harrow, and became known as Powell & Sons (Whitefriars) Ltd.

In the post-war period, the influence of Scandinavian design on British glassware became increasingly evident in work such as that of William Wilson and Geoffrey Baxter, who joined the company in 1954. Baxter's moulded, organic pieces showed the impact of Scandinavian glassware on British design, as seen in particular in the popular Textured Range of 1967. Tree bark, nails and other objects were introduced into the moulds to make the designs more interesting, but it was the colours that drew particular attention. Initially available in cinnamon, indigo and willow, with blue and tangerine introduced two years later, the range was an immediate hit. Whitefriars made textured domestic glass through the 1970s, notably the 1972 Glacier Range, but the factory closed in 1980.

☞ **Items to look out for**

Geoffrey Baxter's Drunken Bricklayer Vase. A small vase costs £250 (US $400), a medium one £400 (US $640) and a large one over £600 (US $960). The Banjo Vase costs about £600 (US $960) and the TV Vase about £250 (US $400).

1970s' Textured Vases, unless rare, usually cost £50 to £80 (US $80–130), depending on colour and size. Larger items from this period can cost over £200 (US $320).

🎔 **Top Tips**

Textured Whitefriars Glass from the 1970s (see opposite) is often cheaper than 1960s' examples.

Not all Whitefriars Glass is marked and as a result many sellers are unwilling to use the Whitefriars label so you may pick up a bargain if you know your stuff.

www **Websites**

The Collectors Site for Whitefriars Glass
www.whitefriars.com

20th Century Glass
www.20thcenturyglass.com

Venini Bolle Vases
Tapio Wirkkala

Venini has been making some of the world's most beautiful glass for decades on the famous Venetian island of Murano. It has attracted some of the most innovative designers, including Finnish master Tapio Wirkkala, who produced the Bolle Vases.

Today the largest and most successful of the Murano glassworks, Venini attracted the cream of master glass makers from its beginning. The brainchild of antiques dealer Giacomo Cappelin and lawyer Paolo Venini, the company was established in 1921 as Cappelin Venini & C. It gained its reputation for avant-garde design under the direction of painter Vittorio Zecchin, exhibiting at the 1922 Biennale in Venice. In 1925, the company was restructured as VSM Venini & C, this time directed by sculptor Napoleone Martinuzzi.

By the 1930s, Paolo Venini was becoming more and more involved in the artistic output of the company, which attracted some of the leading artists, designers and architects of the day. Finnish artist Tapio Wirkkala produced the stunning Bolle Vases for Venini in 1968. Wirkkala designed these vases using two different types of glass, which were worked separately and fused to produce one beautiful end product. This technique, called incalmo, was perfected by the master glassworkers at Venini. Featuring five pieces in the colourways green/yellow/violet, grey/amethyst, grey/aquamarine, straw yellow/apple green and straw yellow/red, Wirkkala's Bolle Vases are available as a set or individually.

☞ **Items to look out for**

Bolle Vases sell from between £850 and £1550 (US $1,360-2,480) separately and £5150 (US $8,240) for a set of five.

💡 **Top Tips**

The five Wirkkala Bolle Vases come in specific colourways: green/yellow/violet; grey/amethyst; grey/aquamarine; straw yellow/apple green; and straw yellow/red.

📖 **Websites**

Venini
www.venini.com

Clarice Cliff

Instantly recognizable, Clarice Cliff's unique designs and style truly typify the Art Deco period. The startling contrast between design classics such as Crocus and Lugano and shapes like her Yo Yo Vase is extraordinary.

Clarice Cliff's beautiful pottery attracted a mass market audience in the 1930s and its brilliance and beauty make it highly collectable even today.

She was born in 1899 in Tunstall, a suburb of Stoke-on-Trent, Staffordshire, and joined A.J.Wilkinson's Royal Staffordshire Pottery at the age of 17. There, her skill as an artist brought her to the fore and she was sent to study at the Royal College of Art in London in 1927. She set up a studio in Wilkinson's Newport Pottery, where she produced her striking Art Deco-influenced designs on Newport's blank ware.

In 1927–8, Cliff introduced her Bizarre Range, designs first made up of diamonds, oblongs and squares painted in crude colours. Despite its striking and different look – and to the surprise of the sales team – Bizarre sold very quickly. Her most collectable ranges – such as Bizarre, Fantasque and Appliqué – were produced between 1927 and 1936. Cliff's work began to become collectable in the 1960s and '70s, but shot up in value in the 1980s and '90s. The market remains extremely buoyant today.

Cliff died in 1972. Her centenary year was 1999 and was celebrated with an exhibition at the Wedgwood Museum in Stoke-on-Trent. The exhibition was visited by more than 100,000 people, including some of Cliff's original painters, by then all over 80 years of age.

☞ **Items to look out for**

Minor pieces of Crocus start at £30 (US $50) but, depending on the design, you can pay up to £20,000 (US $32,000).

Elaborate patterns, such as geometric designs, are prized. Expect to pay upwards of £700 (US $1,120).

Landscape scenes are desirable, as are Art Deco designs. These cost upwards of £200 (US $320).

💡 **Top Tips**

The more classically Art Deco the shape, the more valuable the piece. Bonjour and Stamford are good shapes to look for.

Cliff's work from the late 1920s/early 1930s often had handwritten back stamps.

Some 1930s' work was not stamped at all, so look out for such pieces.

📟 **Websites**

Clarice Cliff site
www.claricecliff.co.uk

Susie Cooper

Like Clarice Cliff, Susie Cooper was committed to the idea that ceramics could be attractive but affordable. She created ergonomic and streamlined shapes as seen in ranges such as Kestrel, Falcon and Curlew, all popular with collectors.

Susie Cooper came to notice while working for the potter A.E. Gray, in Staffordshire, in the 1920s. The desire to have control over the shape as well as the pattern design of her work led Cooper to set up her own company in 1929. Initially buying in whiteware, she painted it with her own designs and stamped it with 'Susie Cooper Productions' enclosed in a black triangle. By the 1930s, this mark had been replaced by the more recognizable leaping deer.

In the late 1920s and early 1930s, Cooper's work was often brightly coloured and geometric. These designs reflected the modernist themes of the time, but soon Cooper was introducing new shapes and designs, such as bands of colour and polka dots. She also utilized lithographs to create ranges such as the Kestrel Shape, with its clean lines and nod to Art Deco. Like Clarice Cliff, Cooper understood that the domestic market wanted well-designed but practical ceramics.

The 1950s were notable for Cooper's bone china designs. In 1966, she sold her company to Wedgwood, for whom she worked until 1972, producing further distinctive designs, such as Carnaby Daisy, based on a daisy pattern, and Cornpoppy. Cooper retired to the Isle of Man in the mid-1980s but continued designing until her death in 1995.

☞ **Items to look out for**

Many collectors prefer Cooper's 1920s and 1930s' Art Deco work. A Kestrel Coffee Set (c.1932) with pot, sugar bowl, milk jug and six coffee cups and saucers can start at £745 (US $1,190). A Carnaby Daisy set of six cups and saucers (1968) can start at £350 (US $560).

💡 **Top Tips**

Be careful when buying Gray's pottery as not everything has a 'Designed by Susie Cooper' mark.

It is possible to buy items for less than £10 (US $16) on sites such as eBay. Check the descriptions and seller's rating carefully.

Kestrel Shape was reissued in the late 1980s but only appeared in the patterns Yellow Daisy, Pink Fern and Pollen Dot.

🌐 **Websites**

Grays Pottery
www.grayspottery.co.uk
Susie Cooper site
www.susiecooper.net

Also See

■ Clarice Cliff, pages 186–7

Gunnar Nylund

Although ceramicist Gunnar Nylund originally worked in his native Denmark, where he established Saxbo, it is for his work at the Swedish company Rörstrand that he is best known. He was a leading designer there between 1930 and 1958.

Gunnar Nylund trained as an architect, but he is famous as a talented ceramicist. Much of Nylund's best work is almost architectural in form, showing a recognizable grace, simplicity and elegance.

In the early 1920s, Nylund began to work for porcelain manufacturer Bing & Grøndahl in Copenhagen, before breaking away with fellow Dane Nathalie Krebs to start a workshop, which they called Saxbo. There, Nylund diligently created streamlined modernist stoneware, while Krebs concentrated on developing the rich finishing glazes. The Saxbo work from this period quickly gained critical and popular attention after it was exhibited at the interior-design shop Svenskt Tenn in Stockholm in 1930.

In the same year, however, Nylund was recruited by Rörstrand and it was for this Swedish company that his most recognized designs were produced. Nylund's work was diverse: he experimented in a range of materials and produced everything from unique designs in mall glazed stoneware and impressive sculptures in the rough chamotte (also known as grog or firesand) to moderately priced miniature vases and bowls and utility tableware in porcelain.

Nylund left Sweden in 1958, returning to Denmark, where he became art director of the Nymölle Pottery. In his later years, he had his own studio in Malmö.

☞ **Items to look out for**

Nylund and Krebs's Saxbo work from the late 1920s.

It is still possible to find Nylund's work from the 1950s (see opposite) for reasonable prices. Prices for an Ash Three-Winged Bowl with Nylund and Rörstrand's mark can start at £55 (US $88).

💡 **Top Tips**

Some Saxbo pieces are not signed by Nylund but are still very collectable, particularly from the years 1929–30.

The incised 'R', three crown marks and 'GN' often mark Nylund's Rörstrand work.

🌐 **Websites**

Rörstrand
www.rorstrand.se

Royal Copenhagen

Denmark held its own in the ceramics stakes through the output of the talented designers who worked at Royal Copenhagen. They created a diverse range of high-quality and cutting-edge designs that often had mass-market appeal.

Royal Copenhagen has its origins in the Royal Danish Porcelain Manufactory, whose doors opened in 1775 and was, until 1868, run by the Danish Royal Family. The current Royal Copenhagen was created by the merging of the Danish porcelain factory Bing & Grøndahl with Royal Copenhagen in 1987.

During the 20th century, the company employed a series of designers who brought Danish ceramics design to the attention of the wider world, building on Royal Copenhagen's already strong reputation. Nils Thorsson joined the company in 1912 and was one of its most prolific designers and also its artistic director from 1949. Thorsson created some of the company's best-known ranges, including Solberg in the 1930s and Baca in the 1960s. The latter range was decorated by various artists, including Inge-Lise Sørensen and Marianne Johnson (who also produced the Surreal Series for the company).

In addition, Royal Copenhagen produced the work of Axel Salto, one of the most important Danish ceramics designers of the 20th century, from the 1930s until his death in 1961. Salto made expressive and vital pottery, creating pieces with surfaces that rippled with energy. He experimented with Chinese and classic glazes, such as solfatara, and drew inspiration from natural motifs.

☞ **Items to look out for**

Axel Salto's work. Many pieces are held in private collections, such as the c.1950 planter (see opposite).

Nils Thorsson, Inge-Lise Sørensen and Marianne Johnson's work.

💡 **Top Tips**

Salto's work is becoming increasingly expensive. A Living Stone Vase sold for £2,500 (US $4,000) in 2009. A c.1960 26.7x10.8cm (10.5x4.25in) glazed stoneware vase can start at £1,560 (US $2,500), but much of his work is far more pricey. Some of his lithographs start from about £940 (US $1,500).

Thorsson's work can be found for as little as £95 (US $150), although a rare planter can cost £15,600 (US $25,000).

🔳 **Websites**

Royal Copenhagen
www.royalcopenhagen.com

Jessie Tait

Typical of the post-war generation of ceramics artists, Jessie Tait designed stylish pottery aimed at allowing the masses to have beautiful objects at affordable prices. The Zambesi Range is probably her most recognized work.

When Jessie Tait and Terence Conran became designers at the Staffordshire pottery Midwinter, it marked a radical change in British ceramics design. Across the Atlantic Ocean, designers such as Russel Wright and Eva Zeisel were already reacting to changes in the post-war domestic market. British designers, however, had been slower to respond to market need for good-looking and practical ceramics. When Roy Midwinter recognized this demand, Jessie Tait was among the designers he employed to help address this need.

Producing 'must have' goods for an aspirational young generation, Tait designed ware that is still as attractive to modern collectors as it was to the 1950s' audiences who saw and purchased it for the first time. Accordingly, when Roy Midwinter released the Stylecraft Range with television-shaped plates and neat cups, Tait produced its patterns: abstract floral-designed Primavera; Red Domino, with its red rim dotted with white; and the Joan Miro-inspired Fantasy, among other designs.

Zambesi, launched in 1956, is one of Tait's most recognized ranges. Sophisticated and chic, its exotic black-and-white zebra stripe was enlivened by splashes of red (see opposite). Hugely popular at the time, it is still among Tait's most sought-after work.

☞ **Items to look out for**

Zambesi Range – each piece is hand painted. Expect to pay £1,000–1,500 (US $1,600–2,400) for a set.

Midwinter – particularly Primavera and Red Domino; a Homeweave three-piece tea set can start at £79 (US $125).

🍲 **Top Tips**

Auction sites, such as eBay, are still the best place to pick up Jessie Tait bargains, such as soup tureens or single plates.

Examine Midwinter goods carefully. You may be picking up a Conran design rather than a Tait.

🌐 **Websites**

Deco-etcetera
www.deco-etcetera.com

Upsala Ekeby

Originally founded as a brick and tile manufacturing company, Upsala Ekeby became famous for its innovative ceramics through the work of designers such as Sven Erik Skawonius, Ingrid Atterberg, Mari Simmulson and Hjördis Oldfors.

Established in the 1880s, Upsala Ekeby only began to be noticed for its range of products after Anna-Lisa Thomson and Sven Erik Skawonius were hired to design their ceramics.

In the 1940s, Mari Simmulson and Ingrid Atterberg joined the company. All of their designs are today very collectable among Scandinavian ceramics enthusiasts. Simmulson and Atterberg, in particular, produced modern, graphic pieces that had popular appeal. Atterberg was a driving force at Upsala Ekeby between 1944 and 1963.

The 1950s were Upsala Ekeby's most celebrated period in terms of ceramics design and many works from that period can be seen in museums around the world, including the Victoria and Albert Museum (V&A) in London. During this period, Hjördis Oldfors was one of the company's most important designers, working there between 1952 and 1959. Her work is very distinctive and combines elegance with balanced shapes and abstract graphic design, as seen in the Pingvin Vase (1954) and her stoneware Kokos Range (see opposite), released between 1954 and 1958. The name 'Kokos' comes from the Swedish word for coconut and the range has a matt dark-brown finish with deep cuts of a bright yellow glaze. Oldfors signed her work with an 'Hj' in a circle.

☞ Items to look out for

Work by Ingrid Atterberg has become very collectable but is still affordable. A thick ceramic slab tray with a bright geometric grid (20.5x33cm/8x13in) sold for just over £63 (US $100) in 2011.

♟ Top Tips

Look out for 'UE SWEDEN' in a circle on the base of Upsala Ekeby goods.

The Pingvin Vase is quite rare and even on eBay can sell for more than £345 (US $550).

▭ Websites

Hi+lomodern
www.hiandlomodern.com

Kirkmodern
www.kirkmodern.com

Stig Lindberg

One of Scandinavia's most prolific ceramicists, Stig Lindberg was the chief designer of Swedish ceramics manufacturer Gustavsberg from 1949. His work is celebrated and can be found in museum collections around the world.

After the Second World War, Scandinavian ceramics began to gain a reputation for their beautiful and original designs. At the forefront was Gustavsberg, in Sweden, then under the directorship of Wilhelm Kåge. Stig Lindberg joined the company as a faience painter in the 1930s and was greatly influenced by Kåge, who had created the very successful Argenta Range for the company.

When Lindberg replaced Kåge in 1949, he quickly built up a reputation as a master designer. In the 1950s and '60s, his output was extraordinarily diverse, from one-off pieces to mass-manufactured work. Lindberg became known for the humour and light-heartedness of his designs and his use of motifs, produced in the greens, ochres, blues, reds and blacks popular in the post-war period. A sculptural influence is also evident in the pieces he produced during that time, whether it be the lovely fluid forms of the Veckla Range or in the beauty of a rare black earthenware bird house, both from the 1950s.

Among the best known of Lindberg's work is the Berså Range, produced by Gustavsberg between 1960 and 1974. The stylized green leaf design and slightly geometric shape of the pieces made it very popular with consumers at the time and has also brought it to the attention of collectors in recent years.

☞ Items to look out for

The Berså Range (see opposite) is much sought after. A milk jug alone can cost as much as £128 (US $205).

♥ Top Tips

Be careful not to put Berså in a dishwasher. There are many faded examples to be found on sites such as eBay.

Stig Lindberg's work is usually marked with 'Stig L', the mark of a hand and a very large 'G'.

Websites

Stig Lindberg
www.stiglindberg.info

Denby

The English pottery Denby is more than 200 years old. The 1960s saw a range of innovative wares, such as Arabesque by Gill Pemberton, which heralded the new age of beautifully designed oven and tableware ceramics.

When Denby began trading as Joseph Bourne in 1809, the name for which it was known for more than a century, it produced salt-glazed bottles in a range of sizes. Over the decades, its output increased to include the D-shaped Footwarmer of the early 20th century, aimed at keeping motorists (then a relatively new group of travellers) warm, the Cottage Blue Range, the iconically shaped Nevva-Drip Teapot ('pours perfectly … and never drips') of the 1920s and the first hand-decorated tableware ranges of the 1950s, such as Albert Colledge's Greenwheat, which was so popular that it was produced until the 1970s.

Denby really began to come into its own in the 1960s and the goods from this era are of particular interest to design-savvy collectors. After a trip to Russia in 1962, designer Gill Pemberton was inspired to introduce the red and gold hand-painted stylish Arabesque Range. It was originally called Samarkand but its name was changed when a British competitor used the same name. However, some of it was marketed in the United States as Samarkand. It was discontinued in 1984.

Glyn Colledge, Albert Colledge's son, also worked at Denby and was one of its most influential designers. In 1950, he replaced his father as head of the hand-painted stoneware department and Denby's popular Danesby Range was renamed Glyn Ware in his honour.

☞ Items to look out for

Early Glynbourne Vases that have Glyn Colledge's signature incised. Due to firing difficulties, this was replaced by an applied signature until the 1970s.

Denby's Samarkand pottery.

♦ Top Tips

Denby Arabesque can still be picked up very cheaply on internet sites and in vintage shops for as little as £10 (US $16) for an egg cup or a coaster, but try your local car boot sale as well.

▭ Websites

Denby
www.denby.co.uk
Denby China Find
www.denbychinafind.co.uk

Troika

The Cornwall-based pottery Troika opened its doors in 1963. The dream of innovative artists Benny Sirota, Leslie Illsley and Jan Thompson, Troika had a distinctive style that has made it very sought after by ceramics collectors.

Troika Pottery was based on Wheal Dream, a street near Porthgwidden Beach in St Ives, in what had been the Powell and Wells Pottery. Originally the artists Sirota, Illsley and Thompson worked together, but Thompson was bought out in 1965.

In 1970, the pottery relocated several kilometres away to an old salting house, Fragden Place in Newlyn, where it expanded its production, range and staff. The 1970s were arguably the pottery's halcyon years.

Initially, the designers utilized the doorknob and tile blanks from the old pottery but quickly moved on to create their own moulds. Sirota experimented with glazes and surface textures while Illsley, who had trained as a sculptor, designed the works. Their collaboration resulted in the textured surfaces, sculpted shapes and finish for which Troika became so famous. The Cornish landscape informed the abstract decorative features of the textured pieces, which were produced in combinations of earthy, muted colours.

Troika began to supply the upmarket design store Heal's in London in the late 1970s. Sirota left in 1980, but Illsey carried on the company until 1983, when it was forced to close its doors after a decline in the market. Today, Troika's distinctive work is very appealing to ceramics collectors.

☞ **Items to look out for**

The original Coffin Vase.

Ann Lewis's work (c.1966–72). A rectangular vase (22.25cm/8.75in) can go for £285 (US $450).

 Top Tips

Look out for the hand-painted Troika mark on the base, often followed by the designer's initials, such as JB (John Bedding) or SB (Stella Benjamin).

Troika's work is distinctive and collectors should ask themselves: Is the piece made from moulded earthenware? Does it have a textured surface?

 Websites

Cornish Ceramics
www.cornishceramics.com

Glossary of Designers

Alvar Aalto (1898–1976). Finnish architect and furniture designer. **See Furniture:** 41 Paimio. **Household:** Tea Trolley 901. **Glass:** Savoy Vase.

Eero Aarnio (1932–). Finnish furniture designer. **See Furniture:** Bubble Chair.

Tony Alfström (1972–). Finnish industrial designer. **See Household:** Warm.

Edward Barber (1969–). British furniture and interior designer of Barber Osgerby. **See Furniture:** Loop Table.

Geoffrey Baxter (1922–95). British glass designer. **See Glass:** Whitefriars Glass.

Robert Dudley Best (1892–1984). British industrial designer. **See Lighting:** BL1 Table Lamp (Bestlite).

Max Bill (1908–94). Swiss architect, industrial designer and sculptor. **See Household:** Wall Clock 32/0389.

Hugo Blomberg (1897–1994). Swedish product designer. **See Household:** Ericofon.

Kay Bojesen (1886–1958). Danish product designer. **See Household:** Wooden Monkey.

Marcel Breuer (1902–81). Hungarian-born American architect and furniture designer. **See Furniture:** B3 (Wassily) Chair; Isokon Long Chair.

George Carwardine (1887–1947). British lighting designer. **See Lighting:** Anglepoise 1227.

Achille Castiglioni (1918–2002). Italian furniture and lighting designer. **See Lighting:** Arco Floor Light; Snoopy Table Lamp; Taraxacum 88 Chandelier.

Pier Giacomo Castiglioni (1913–68). Italian furniture and lighting designer. **See Lighting:** Arco Floor Light; Snoopy Table Lamp.

Antonio Citterio (1950–). Italian architect and furniture designer. **See Furniture:** Charles Sofa.

Clarice Cliff (1899–1972). British ceramics designer. **See Ceramics:** Clarice Cliff.

Glyn Colledge (1922–2000). British ceramics designer. **See Ceramics:** Denby.

Joe Colombo (1930–71). Italian furniture and product designer. **See Lighting:** Spider 291.

Susie Cooper (1902–95). British ceramics designer. **See Ceramics:** Susie Cooper.

Nanna Ditzel (1923–2005). Danish furniture and textile designer. **See Furniture:** Egg.

Tom Dixon (1959–). British furniture designer. **See Furniture:** S Chair.

Charles (1907–78) and **Ray** (1912–88) **Eames**. American furniture designers. **See Furniture:** LCW (Lounge Chair Wood); La Chaise; LAR, DAR and RAR; ESU Bookshelf; Model 670 and Model 671 (Lounge Chair and Ottoman); Soft Pad Chair. **Household:** Hang-It-All.

Tias Eckhoff (1926–). Norwegian furniture and product designer. **See Household:** Maya.

Christian (1921–94) and **Grethe** (1922–) **Flensted**. Danish product designers. **See Household:** Flensted Mobile.

Kaj Franck (1911–89). Finnish glass designer. **See Household:** Teema. **Glass:** Nuutajärvi Notsjö.

Pøul Henningsen (1894–1967). Danish architect and designer. **See Lighting:** PH5; PH Artichoke.

Matthew Hilton (1957–). British furniture designer. **See Furniture:** Balzac Armchair and Ottoman.

Arne Jacobsen (1902–71). Danish architect and furniture designer. **See Furniture:** Model 3107 (Series 7); Egg Chair; Swan Sofa. **Household:** Cutlery; Cylinda Tea Service. **Lighting:** AJ Light.

Pierre Jeanneret (1896–1967). Swiss architect and furniture designer. **See Furniture:** LC3 Sofa (Grand Confort); Chaise Longue LC4.

Finn Juhl (1912–89). Danish furniture designer. **See Furniture:** NV-45; Chieftain Chair. **Household:** Teak Bowl.

Brian Keaney (1974–). Irish industrial designer. **See Household:** Warm.

Poul Kjærholm (1929–80). Danish furniture designer. **See Furniture:** PK24 Chaise Longue (Hammock).

Florence Knoll (1917–). American architect and furniture designer. **See Furniture:** 2-Seater Settee.

Herbert Krenchel (1922–). Danish engineer and product designer. **See Household:** Krenit Bowl.

Le Corbusier (Charles-Édouard Jeanneret-Gris; 1887–1965). Swiss/French architect and furniture designer. **See Furniture:** LC3 Sofa (Grand Confort); Chaise Longue LC4.

Stig Lindberg (1916–82). Swedish glass, ceramics and textile designer. **See Ceramics:** Stig Lindberg.

Dietrich Lubs (1938–). German industrial designer. **See Household:** ET44.

Per Lütken (1916-98). Danish glass maker. **See Glass:** Holmegaard.

Ralph Lysell (1907–87). Swedish product designer. **See Household:** Ericofon.

Enzo Mari (1932–). Italian furniture and product designer. **See Household:** Calendario Bilancia.

Ludwig Mies van der Rohe (1886–1969). German architect and furniture designer. **See Furniture:** Barcelona Chair; Brno chair (MR50).

Jasper Morrison (1959–). British furniture and product designer. **See Furniture:** Low Pad.

George Nelson (1908–86). American furniture designer. **See Furniture:** Marshmallow Sofa. Household: Sunburst Clock.

Isamu Noguchi (1904–88). Japanese/American sculptor. **See Furniture:** Noguchi Table (IN-50).

Gunnar Nylund (1904–97). Danish/Finnish ceramics designer. **See Ceramics:** Gunnar Nylund.

Jay Osgerby (1969–). British furniture and interior designer of Barber Osgerby. **See Furniture:** Loop Table.

Verner Panton (1926–98). Danish furniture and lighting designer. **See Furniture:** Panton Stacking Chair. **Lighting:** Moon Lamp; FlowerPot; VP Globe; Spiral Triple SP3.

Pierre Paulin (1926–2009). French furniture designer. **See Furniture:** Ribbon Chair.

Charlotte Perriand (1903–99). French architect and furniture designer. **See Furniture:** LC3 Sofa (Grand Confort); Chaise Longue LC4.

Jens Quistgaard (1919–2008). Danish industrial designer. **See Household:** Congo Ice Bucket.

Dieter Rams (1932–). German industrial designer. **See Furniture:** 606 Universal Shelving System. Household: ET44.

Lilly Reich (1885–1947). German furniture designer. **See Furniture:** Barcelona Chair; Brno Chair (MR50).

Egon Riss (1901–64). Austrian architect. **See Furniture:** Isokon Penguin Donkey.

Eero Saarinen (1910–61). Finnish–American architect and furniture designer. **See Furniture:** Womb Chair; Tulip (Model 150); Tulip Table.

Axel Salto (1889–1961). Danish ceramics designer. **See Ceramics:** Royal Copehagen.

Richard Sapper (1932–). Germany/Italian industrial designer. **See Household:** 9091 Kettle. Lighting: Tizio 35.

Gino Sarfatti (1912–84). Italian lighting designer. **See Lighting:** 2097 Chandelier.

Timo Sarpaneva (1926–2006). Finnish glass designer. **See Household:** Sarpaneva Casserole.

Philippe Starck (1949–). French architect and appliance designer. **See Lighting:** ARA.

Jessie Tait (1928–2010). British ceramics designer. **See Ceramics:** Jessie Tait.

Has Gösta Thames (1916–). Swedish product designer. **See Household:** Ericofon.

Wilhelm Wagenfeld (1900–90). German glass and metalware designer. **See Household:** Tea Service.

Hans J. Wegner (1914–2007). Danish furniture designer. **See Furniture:** Round Chair; Wishbone Chair; Teddy Bear Chair (PP19); Valet Chair (PP250); Oxchair.

Tapio Wirkkala (1915–85). Finnish glass designer. **See Glass:** Venini Bolle Vases.

Komin Yamada (1947–). Japanese industrial designer. **See Household:** Global Knife.

Sori Yanagi (1915–). Japanese furniture designer. **See Furniture:** Butterfly Stool. Household: Teapot.

Index

Acknowledgements

Fletcher Sibthorp would like to thank everyone at New Holland, especially his publisher Aruna Vasudevan for commissioning *Collectables* and for her outstanding contribution to the text and Susannah Jayes for her excellent picture research. He would also like to thank the designers and manufacturers for their advice and feedback in producing this book, and his wife, Nicci.

Picture credits: B3 (Wassily) Chair – Marcel Breuer: Courtesy of Knoll: p.10; LC3 Sofa (Grand Confort) – Le Corbusier/Jeanneret/Perriand: Courtesy of Cassina/© FLC/ADAGP, Paris, and DACS, London, 2011: p.13; Chaise Longue LC4 – Le Corbusier/Jeanneret/Perriand: Courtesy of Knoll/© FLC/ADAGP, Paris, and DACS, London: p.14; Barcelona Chair – Mies van der Rohe/Reich: Courtesy of Knoll: p.17; Brno Chair (MR50) – Mies van der Rohe/Reich: © 2011. Digital image, The Museum of Modern Art, New York/Scala, Florence (Gift of Knoll International, Inc., USA. Acc. n.: 412.1976): p.18: 41 Paimio – Alvar Aalto: Produced by Artek: Courtesy of SCP/© DACS 2011: p.21; Isokon Long Chair – Marcel Beuer: Courtesy of Isokon Plus: p.22; Isokon Penguin Donkey – Egon Riss: Courtesy of Isokon Plus: p.6, p.25; LCW (Lounge Chair Wood) – Charles and Ray Eames: Courtesy of Herman Miller: p.26; NV-45 – Finn Juhl: Courtesy of Skandium: p.29; Round Chair – Hans J. Wegner: Courtesy of PP Møbler: p.30; Noguchi Table (IN-50) – Isamu Noguchi: Courtesy of Herman Miller: p.33; Womb Chair – Eero Saarinen: Courtesy of Knoll: p.34; La Chaise – Charles and Ray Eames: © Vitra: p.37; LAR, DAR and RAR – Charles and Ray Eames: RAR by Charles and Ray Eames, produced by Modernica: Courtesy of SCP: p.38; Chieftain Chair – Finn Juhl: Courtesy of Skandium: p.41; Wishbone Chair – Hans J. Wegner: Courtesy of Carl Hansen & Son: p.42; ESU Bookshelf – Charles and Ray Eames: Courtesy of The Conran Shop: p.45; Teddy Bear Chair (PP19) – Hans J. Wegner: Courtesy of PP Møbler: p.46; Valet Chair (PP250) – Hans J. Wegner: Courtesy of PP Møbler: p.49; 2-Seater Settee – Florence Knoll: Courtesy of Knoll: p.50; Butterfly Stool – Sori Yanagi: Produced by Vitra: p.53; Model 3107 (Series 7) – Arne Jacobsen: Courtesy of Fritz Hansen: p.54; Tulip Chair (Model 150) – Eero Saarinen: Courtesy of Knoll: p.57; Tulip Table – Eero Saarinen: Courtesy of The Conran Shop: p.58; Model 670 and Model 671 (Lounge Chair and Ottoman) – Charles and Ray Eames: Courtesy of The Conran Shop: p.61; Marshmallow Sofa – George Nelson: Courtesy of Herman Miller: p.62; Egg Chair – Arne Jacobsen: Courtesy of Fritz Hansen: p.65; Swan Sofa – Arne Jacobsen: Courtesy of Fritz Hansen: p.66; Egg – Nanna Ditzel: Courtesy of Studio Prada: p.69; Oxchair – Hans J. Wegner: Courtesy of Erik Jøergensen: p.70; 606 Universal Shelving System – Dieter Rams: Courtesy of Vitsoe: p.73; PK24 Chaise Longue (Hammock) – Poul Kjærholm: Courtesy of Fritz Hansen: p.74; Ribbon Chair – Pierre Paulin: Courtesy of Artifort: p.77; Bubble Chair – Eero Aarnio: Courtesy of Eero Aarnio: p.4, p.78; Panton Stacking Chair – Verner Panton: © Vitra: p.81; Soft Pad Chair – Charles and Ray Eames – Courtesy of Herman Miller: p.82; S Chair – Tom Dixon: Courtesy of Cappellini: p.85; Balzac Armchair and Ottoman – Matthew Hilton: Courtesy of Heal's: p.86; Charles Sofa – Antonio Citterio: Courtesy of Bebitalia: p.89; Loop Table – Barber Osergby – Courtesy of Isokon Plus: p.90; Low Pad – Jasper Morrison: Courtesy of Cappellini: p.93; Tea Service – Wilhelm Wagenfeld: Courtesy of Werbewelt: p.94; Tea Trolley

901 – Alvar Aalto: Courtesy of Artek/© DACS 2011: p.97; Sunburst Clock – George Nelson: Courtesy of Heal's: p.98; Europiccola – La Pavoni: © Richard Jenkins Photography 2011: p.101; Wooden Monkey – Kay Bojesen: Courtesy of Rosendahl: p.102; Teak Bowl – Finn Juhl: Courtesy of Dansk Møbelkunst: p.105; Krenit Bowl – Herbert Krenchel: Courtesy of Normann-Copenhagen: p.106; Hang-It-All – Charles and Ray Eames: Courtesy of Heal's: p.7, p.109; Ericofon – Blomberg/Lysell/Gösta Thames: © Richard Jenkins Photography 2011: p.110; Flensted Mobile – Christian and Grethe Flensted: Courtesy of Flensted Mobiles: p.113; Teapot – Sori Yanagi: © Biscuit Ltd 2011: p.114; Cutlery – Arne Jacobsen: Courtesy of Georg Jensen: p.117; Wall Clock 32/0389 – Max Bill: Courtesy of Junghans: p.118; Sarpaneva Casserole – Timo Sarpaneva: Courtesy of Iittala: p.121; Calendario Bilancia – Enzo Mari: Courtesy of Danese Milano: p.122; Congo Ice Bucket – Jens Quistgaard: © Biscuit Ltd 2011: p.125; Maya – Tias Eckhoff: Courtesy of Stelton: p.126; Cylinda Tea Service – Arne Jacobsen: Courtesy of Stelton: p.129; ET44 – Dieter Rams and Dietrich Lubs: Alamy/Chris Mattison: p.130; Teema – Kaj Franck: Courtesy of Iittala: p.9 (r), p.133; 9091 Kettle – Richard Sapper: Courtesy of Connox GmbH: p.134; Global Knife – Komin Yamada: Courtesy of Grunwerg Ltd: p.137; Warm – Brian Keaney and Tony Alfström: Courtesy of Tonfisk Design Oy: p.138; BL1 Table Light (BestLite) – Robert Dudley Best: Courtesy of GUBI A/S: p. 8, p.141; Anglepoise 1227 – George Carwardine: Produced by Anglepoise: Courtesy of SCP: p.142; AJ Light – Arne Jacobsen: Courtesy of Louis Poulsen Lighting: p.145; PH5 – Pøul Henningsen: Courtesy of Louis Poulsen Lighting: p.146; PH Artichoke – Pøul Henningsen: Courtesy of Louis Poulsen Lighting: p.149; 2097 Chandelier – Gino Sarfatti: Courtesy of Flos: p.150; Moon Lamp – Verner Panton: Courtesy of VerPan ApS: p.153; Arco Floor Light – Achille and Pier Giacomo Castiglioni: Courtesy of Flos: p.154; Spider 291 – Joe Colombo: Courtesy of Oluce S.r.l: p.157; Snoopy Table Lamp – Achille and Pier Giacomo Castiglioni: Courtesy of Flos: p.158; FlowerPot – Verner Panton: Courtesy of Heal's: p.161; VP Globe – Verner Panton: Courtesy of VerPan ApS: p.162; Spiral Triple SP3 – Verner Panton: Courtesy of VerPan ApS: p.165; Tizio 35 – Richard Sapper: Courtesy of Artemide: p.166; Taraxacum 88 Chandelier – Achille Castiglioni: Courtesy of Flos: p.169; ARA – Phillippe Stark: Courtesy of Flos: p.170; Savoy Vase – Alvar Aalto: Courtesy of Iittala/© DACS 2011: p.9 (l), p.173; Nuutajärvi Notsjö – Kaj Franck: Courtesy of Peter Hattaway: p.174; Holmegaard – Per Lütken: Art-of-Glass: p.177; Orrefors: Jacksons.se: p.178; Riihimäki – Riihimäen Lasi Oy: Art-of-Glass: p.181; Whitefriars Glass – Geoffrey Baxter: Art-of-Glass: p.182; Venini Bolle Vases – Tapio Wirkkala: Courtesy of Venini S.p.A: p.185; Clarice Cliff: Alamy/Sue Walsham: p.186; Susie Cooper: Grays Pottery: p.189; Gunnar Nylund: Rörstrand Museum: p.190; Royal Copenhagen: The Bridgeman Art Library/Private Collection/Photo © Christie's Images/© DACS 2011: p.193; Jessie Tait: V&A Images: p.194; Upsala Ekeby: Courtesy of Geoff Kirk: p.197; Stig Lindberg: Courtesy of Gustavsbergs Porslinsfabrik: p.198; Denby: Ray Garrod: p.201; Troika: Art-of-Glass: p.202. Every effort has been made to contact copyright holders, but should there be any omissions, New Holland Publishers would be pleased to insert the appropriate acknowledgement in any subsequent printing of this publication.